craft **workshop**

# beads

craft **workshop**

# beads

The art of beadwork in 25 beautiful projects

## Isabel Stanley

photography by Peter Williams

**southwater**

THIS EDITION IS PUBLISHED BY SOUTHWATER

DISTRIBUTED IN THE UK BY
THE MANNING PARTNERSHIP
251–253 LONDON ROAD EAST
BATHEASTON, BATH BA1 7RL
TEL. 01225 852 727
FAX 01225 852 852

PUBLISHED IN THE USA BY
ANNESS PUBLISHING INC.
27 WEST 20TH STREET
SUITE 504, NEW YORK NY 10011
FAX 212 807 6813

DISTRIBUTED IN CANADA BY
GENERAL PUBLISHING
895 DON MILLS ROAD
400–402 PARK CENTRE
TORONTO, ONTARIO M3C 1W3
TEL. 416 445 3333
FAX 416 445 5991

DISTRIBUTED IN AUSTRALIA BY
SANDSTONE PUBLISHING
UNIT 1, 360 NORTON STREET
LEICHHARDT, NEW SOUTH WALES 2040
TEL. 02 9560 7888
FAX 02 9560 7488

SOUTHWATER IS AN IMPRINT OF
ANNESS PUBLISHING LIMITED
HERMES HOUSE, 88–89 BLACKFRIARS ROAD
LONDON SE1 8HA
TEL. 020 7401 2077; FAX 020 7633 9499

© ANNESS PUBLISHING LIMITED 1997, 2002

PUBLISHER: JOANNA LORENZ
SENIOR EDITOR: LINDSAY PORTER
DESIGNER: LILIAN LINDBLOM
PHOTOGRAPHER: PETER WILLIAMS
STYLIST: GEORGINA RHODES
ILLUSTRATORS: MADELEINE DAVID AND
VANA HAGGERTY
PRODUCTION CONTROLLER: JOANNA KING

PREVIOUSLY PUBLISHED AS *NEW CRAFTS: BEADWORK*

10 9 8 7 6 5 4 3 2 1

# CONTENTS

| | |
|---|---|
| INTRODUCTION | 7 |
| HISTORY OF BEADWORK | 8 |
| GALLERY | 12 |
| BEADS | 16 |
| MATERIALS | 18 |
| EQUIPMENT | 20 |
| BASIC TECHNIQUES | 22 |
| CHINESE NECKLACE | 26 |
| VENETIAN NECKLACE | 28 |
| WRAPPED EARRINGS | 30 |
| BEADED BUTTONS | 32 |
| CORD-BEADED BRACELET | 36 |
| SEQUINNED CHRISTMAS DECORATIONS | 38 |
| DEVORÉ SCARF | 40 |
| WOVEN BRACELET | 43 |
| WALLET | 46 |
| DRAMATIC PAINTED GLOVES | 48 |
| PEARL TIARA | 50 |
| BEAD-TRIMMED CUSHIONS | 52 |
| VELVET BOLSTER CUSHION | 56 |
| DRAWSTRING BAG | 59 |
| CHILD'S SLIPPERS | 62 |
| BOTTLE COLLAR | 65 |
| BEAD CANDLE-HOLDER | 68 |
| MILK JUG COVER | 70 |
| NEEDLEPOINT PHOTOGRAPH ALBUM | 72 |
| SPIRALLED CHANDELIER | 75 |
| FLOWERED FRAME | 78 |
| BEAD CURTAIN | 82 |
| WATERFALL SCREEN | 84 |
| FRINGED LAMPSHADE | 88 |
| BEADED TASSELS | 90 |
| TEMPLATES | 94 |
| SUPPLIERS | 95 |
| INDEX | 96 |

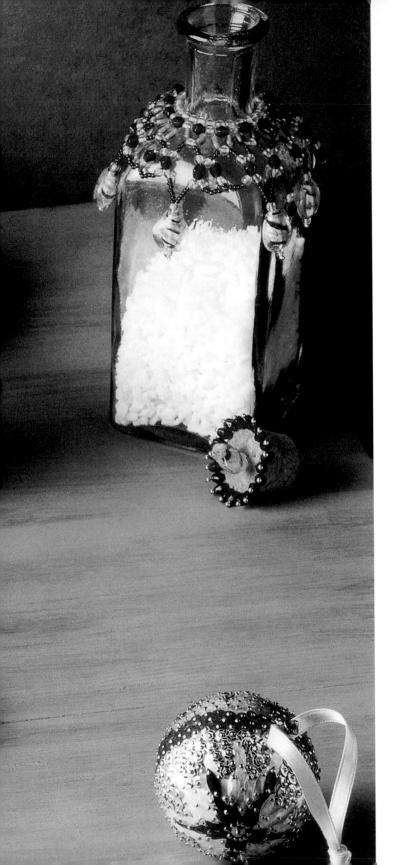

# INTRODUCTION

BEADS ARE SIMPLE DECORATIVE OBJECTS, USUALLY ROUND WITH A HOLE THROUGH THE CENTRE. THEY MAY BE ANY SHAPE AND SIZE AND CAN BE MADE FROM A VARIETY OF MATERIALS. BEADS APPEAL TO BOTH THE EYE AND THE TOUCH. THEY CAN SPARKLE AND SHIMMER AND ADD WEIGHT, RICHNESS AND DEPTH TO ANY WORK. THE FIRST "BEADS" WERE NATURAL FINDS SUCH AS COWRIE SHELLS, FEATHERS, SEEDS, BONES AND WOOD. ALTHOUGH OUR ANCESTORS ADMIRED THESE TRIMMINGS FOR THEIR AESTHETIC QUALITIES, THEY ALSO REGARDED THEM AS TALISMANS IMBUED WITH MYSTICAL POWER. THEY BELIEVED THAT STRINGS OF BEADS COULD PROTECT THE WEARER FROM BALEFUL INFLUENCES AND BRING GOOD FORTUNE. BEADS WERE APPLIED ON THE EDGINGS OF CLOTHES AND COVERS TO ENHANCE THEIR PROTECTIVE QUALITIES. REFLECTIVE SHINY MATERIALS, SUCH AS MICA, SILVER OR BRASS, WERE THOUGHT TO DEFLECT THE EVIL EYE. AS SOCIETIES GREW MORE SOPHISTICATED, NEW MATERIALS AND TECHNIQUES WERE EMPLOYED AND THE ART OF COMMERCIAL BEADMAKING DEVELOPED.

*Left: Beads bring colour and light to almost any object. They can be made from wood, metal, plastic — or even semi-precious stones.*

# HISTORY OF BEADWORK

HISTORICALLY, THE ROLE OF BEADS IN SOCIETY HAS NOT BEEN ONE MERELY OF SIMPLE ORNAMENTATION; THEY HAVE HAD GREAT CULTURAL SIGNIFICANCE. SOME HISTORIANS VIEW THEM AS IMPORTANT ARTEFACTS WHICH REFLECT ECONOMIC, RELIGIOUS AND SOCIAL CONDITIONS. BEADS AND BEADWORK ARE CONSTANTLY CHANGING AND EVOLVING, INFLUENCED BOTH BY FASHION AND TECHNOLOGICAL ADVANCEMENTS.

During the fifteenth century, beads became an important trading currency. European explorers used them as gifts to the indigenous peoples of North America, to initiate friendship and trust. As trade grew between the Native Americans and European merchants, beads and steel needles were exchanged mainly for skins. The imported glass beads soon replaced locally-made bone and shell beads, which had been applied to hides with moosehair and porcupine quills. The Native Americans adopted the fluid floral styles of the foreigners and assimilated them with their own traditional patterns to make beautiful and distinctive moc-casins, pipe bags and skirts.

Commercially-manufactured beads were first introduced to Africa in the fifteenth century by Asians and Europeans. Caravan routes carried the easily portable currency deep into the continent. Merchants traded their glass beads for ivory, skins and even slaves. The more valuable and rare beads quickly became prized possessions, indica-tors of the wealth and status of the wearer. Such was the social significance of certain beads that only upper strata of society were allowed to wear them. The etiquette of beads highlighted other differences apart from social hierarchy. Particular combinations and patterns, as well as the exact position of a given piece, identified the married and the unmarried, or the young and the old. Furthermore, these differences reflected the personal achieve-ments and the birthplace or village of an individual. Certain elaborately beaded

costumes took on special significance and could be worn only by participants during ceremonial performances, weddings and initiation rites.

The Zulu people and the Ndbele-speaking people are particularly well-known for their craftsmanship. Men and women wore necklaces, head bands, belts, bangles and anklets which were made from narrow lengths of beadweaving and beaded, wrapped rope and worn with skins and fur. Women of different status

*Above: A highly decorated Native American beaded cloth sash, together with beaded moccasins and bag. European traders first brought precious glass beads, known as "trade beads" or "pony beads", to the American continent, where they were used as a form of currency. Their trading partners took to them with enthusiasm and integrated them into their existing artistic traditions.*

were distinguished by heavily-beaded girdles, aprons, cloaks and hats. Young women sent colour-and-pattern coded messages in beadwork to their lovers when they were far from home.

In medieval England, the wearing of beads and embroidery had a ceremonial function. The first manufactured beads were made from expensive raw materials, such as precious and semi-precious stones. They were available only to the nobility and the church. Professional embroiderers embellished rich fabrics during the first great period of excellence in English embroidery, the "Opus Anglicum". Drilled pearls and coral were applied with metallic threads to make elaborate and heavy ecclesiastical vestments. These garments must have been a wondrous sight as they sparkled and gleamed in the candle-lit churches. The beads used were so valuable that, when the importance of the church declined, the prized beads were removed and recycled. In the early years of the sixteenth century, some of these stones were then embroidered on to the extravagant costumes of the Tudor nobility. This ushered in a second period of superior craftsmanship. Travelling needlewomen created fabulously rich costumes which were stiff with embroidery and heavy with pearls, spangles, sequins and corals. These gloriously impractical costumes both indicated the importance of the wearer and rendered him or her virtually helpless, needing a coterie of servants to help with dressing and undressing.

In the middle of the seventeenth century, young ladies were encouraged to

*Above: Gloves of white kid embroidered in silver thread and sequins, from the mid-seventeenth century. Such luxury items were a potent sign of status, as they were indicators of both wealth and leisure.*

practise and display their needle and beadworking skills by producing textile jewel boxes as part of their "education". They used a technique now known as stumpwork in which three-dimensional or padded embroidery is worked with silk thread and wool yarn and embellished with small glass beads, spangles and mica. These wonderful caskets feature houses, their elaborately dressed inhabitants and landscape gardens, a particular seventeenth-century preoccupation. These gardens were crammed with exotic flowers, plants and trees, sometimes three-dimensional, and worked with beads threaded on to wire and bent into shape. The bizarre proportions of the features indicate that they were not observed, but copied from illustrations.

During the nineteenth century, embroidery and beadwork became popular hobbies amongst upper- and middle-class ladies. These gentle pursuits were employment enough for privileged women who did not have to work, and the results not only demonstrated the status of the women but also the qualities of femininity, patience and diligence which were then considered desirable.

Victorian ladies also made delicate three-dimensional pieces, such as butterflies, flowers and insects, by threading beads on to wire. They arranged the finished structures as a display under a glass dome or used them to make corsages, tiaras and combs for themselves and as gifts for friends and family.

A passion emerged for using scraps of rich fabrics recycled from favourite dresses to make abstract patchworks. These patchwork quilts were scattered liberally with embroidery stitches, ribbons, buttons, glass beads and sequins.

Beadwork was not just the preserve of women, however – sailors at sea laboured over tokens of affection for their loved ones at home. They made patchwork pincushions using scraps of wool fabric from uniforms and stuffed with sawdust, and spelt out sentimental messages of love and remembrance in beads and sequins threaded on to pins and pressed firmly into the cushion.

The most important craft, however, was Berlinwork, or canvas covered with tent

*Left: Two Victorian Berlinwork waistcoats.*

or cross stitch worked in wool yarn. This craze swept across Europe and America, its popularity based upon the ease with which it could be worked. To take advantage of such a huge market, manufacturers produced thousands of patterns and different-coloured threads and wools. Some patterns featured beadwork. Tiny brass or more often glass beads were stitched in place of yarn to give a shimmery surface on the piece. Different tones were used to give a mottled effect, known as "grisaille work". Homes were filled with bags, tea cosies, covers, bedspreads, slippers, cushions and firescreens, the results of the labours of women.

Throughout the latter half of the nineteenth century there was a fashion for heavily-beaded bodices on evening dresses using jet and small glass beads, and small bags embellished with fringes and tassels.

During the 1920s, women's lives changed rapidly, as they celebrated the end of the Great War, voted for the first time and began to enter the workplace. Fashions reflected this new-found freedom. Narrow low-waisted dresses dripped with rows of fringes of sequins, bugle, drop and glass beads. The shorter styles of dress allowed much greater freedom of movement and the swinging fringes were designed to dazzle whilst dancing the new jazz-age dances. The popularity of beadwork declined with the onset of the Second World War, as rationing meant that clothes became simpler and more austere. In recent years, however, beaded fashions and crafts have had a revival.

Today, beads are produced in great numbers and variety. The incredible choice of beads on the market allows contemporary designers and craft artists to explore the full integral beauty and creative possibilities of beads.

# GALLERY

BEADWORK IS A CENTURIES-OLD CRAFT WITH A RICH HISTORY. TODAY, DESIGNERS AND CRAFTSPEOPLE ARE DRAWN TO THE MEDIUM FOR ITS DECORATIVE QUALITIES AND VERSATILITY. ONCE MORE, BEADS ARE ARE AS LIKELY TO BE FOUND IN HAUTE COUTURE AS IN A CRAFT SHOP. BEADWORK CAN BE MADE FROM ALL TYPES OF MATERIALS, FROM THE REASSURINGLY TRADITIONAL TO THE UNEXPECTEDLY MODERN, AS THESE EXAMPLES OF CONTEMPORARY WORK SHOW.

*Above:* BROOCH AND EARRINGS
The heart-shaped brooch and matching earrings are made from rich velvet fabric worked with gold machine embroidery and finished with decorative beaded fringing.
ISABEL STANLEY

*Right:* CANDLESTICK
This elegant candlestick has a metal base and is embellished with beads strung on wire and wrapped along the shaft.
LIBERTY

*Above left:* BEADED FLOWERS

These decorative beaded flowers are made from crystal chips, garnets and a variety of small and bugle beads, by working out from the centre of the flower and building up the petals. They can be pinned or sewn on to garments or headgear as trims. Draw inspiration from fresh flowers or books.

JANICE MARR

*Above right:* PEARLIZED SEQUINS

If circumstances do not allow you to dress from head to foot in sequins and pearls, then console yourself by adding strategic detail with strips of pearlized sequins. A bead loom is used to create a woven strip studded with fake pearls at intervals for a taste of delicious luxury.

KAREN SPURGIN

*Right:* BEADED CANDLE JAR

Small red beads glow like jewels and allow the warm candlelight to show through the wire structure of this beaded candle jar. In any project that exposes beads to heat, care should be taken to use materials that are neither hazardous nor likely to melt in the heat of a flame.

LIBERTY

*Opposite:* BEADED FRUIT
Scraps of duchess satin and antique velvet have been beaded with cup sequins, small beads and crystal chips. For feel appeal they have been filled with lentils, like little bean bags. The stems are made of twisted jewellery wire and beads, some shaped like leaves.
KAREN SPURGIN

*Right:* BEADED BUSTIER
This stunning piece was worked on a wire base with beads woven in and out of the basic shape.
DIANA LAURIE

*Below left:* SILVER SUN-GLASS FRAMES
Beads are woven in and out of a wire frame for these glamorous glasses. Old necklaces found on market stalls are a good source of beads with distinctive character.
DIANA LAURIE

*Below right:*
DECORATIVE DISCS
Details such as these decorative discs turn a basic fabric into something for a special occasion.
KAREN SPURGIN

# BEADS

MANY CRAFT SHOPS AND MAIL-ORDER SUPPLIERS NOW SPECIALIZE IN BEADS. THERE IS AN ENORMOUS RANGE OF STYLES, SHAPES AND TEXTURES TO CHOOSE FROM — GLASS, METAL, WOOD, MOTHER-OF-PEARL, SEMI-PRECIOUS STONES AND MODERN SYNTHETIC IMITATIONS.

**Bugle beads** Narrow glass tubes, widely available in many sizes, these are particularly effective when used in contrast with small glass beads.

**Crystals** Usually cut glass, these beads have a faceted surface and are available in different shapes such as hearts and diamonds. Use beeswax to protect the beading thread from their sharp edges.

**Drop beads** Shaped like teardrops, these are normally used to finish a strand or area of work.

**Found objects** Many objects such as bottle tops, coins, cogs and driftwood make interesting beads. Use a fine drill to make a hole through the centre. Always use protective eyewear when drilling glass beads.

**Lampwork beads** Made in India, these glass beads are decorated with molten glass trailed in patterns such as leaves or flowers. Some lampwork beads have an insert of silver foil.

**Metal beads** These beads often have sophisticated shapes in brass or copper and may be silver- or gold-plated. They are most often used in jewellery to separate larger beads or at the end of a string.

**Millefiori** Long poles of coloured glass are fused together then sliced into mosaic-like cross sections, literally "thousand flowers". These beads are now also available in plastic.

**Natural materials** Beads made from nuts, seeds, shells, mother-of-pearl and bone are regarded as potent talismans in some countries. Soft wooden beads are more suited to jewellery than embroidery.

**Pearl beads** Artificial pearl beads, with a pearlized finish are available in colours as well as white and ivory.

**Pottery beads** Clay beads were originally made by inserting a wooden stick through the clay shapes. During firing, the stick burnt away to leave a hole. These blue-and-white porcelain beads are of traditional Chinese design.

**Rocailles** These small, slightly flattened glass beads are very popular. Many varieties such as opaque, transparent, metallic and iridescent are available. Sometimes the hole is lined with iridescent or opaque colour, gold or silver.

**Semi-precious stones** Stones such as amber, turquoise, coral and jade are expensive but artificial imitations are also available.

**Sequins** Flat plastic shapes such as stars, flowers and leaves, with one or two holes, are available in different colours and finishes. Originally sequins were made from sheets of gold and silver.

**Small glass beads** Small glass beads, also known as seeds, are used in many beading projects. The are spherical, but, like flatter rocailles, they come in many varieties. They are sometimes sold pre-strung, ready to transfer to a needle.

**Venetian glass beads** These highly decorative beads are from one of the world's most famous beadmaking centres.

**Wound beads** Molten glass is wound around a rotating metal rod to create swirling striped patterns.

| | |
|---|---|
| 1 Rocailles | 11 Lampwork beads |
| 2 Small glass beads | 12 Wound bead |
| 3 Venetian beads | 13 Artificial pearls |
| 4 Millefiori | 14 Crystals |
| 5 Bugle beads | 15 Semi-precious stones |
| 6 Bone beads | — lapis lazuli, etc. |
| 7 Sequins | 16 Pottery beads |
| 8 Drop beads | 17 Wooden beads |
| 9 Pre-strung beads | 18 Metal beads |
| 10 Found objects | 19 Amber |

# MATERIALS

Only a few basic materials are needed in beadwork, depending on the project. The main materials used are, of course, the beads themselves. You may already have many of the other materials in your sewing basket. Many items are available in haberdashery departments or through mail-order suppliers. For further details, see the supplier information at the back of the book.

**Beading thread** This is a special thread designed for beadwork. Alternatively a strong, smooth thread such as polyester is equally effective.

**Beading wire** This is available in gold, copper and silver, and in many diameter sizes. 0.4 mm and 0.6 mm are the most useful sizes. Check that the wire will fit through the hole in the bead.

**Bookbinding fabric** This closely woven cotton fabric has a paper backing that can be glued. It is available from specialist bookbinding suppliers.

**Brass screw binders** Available from specialist bookbinding suppliers, these are used to hold sheaves of paper together to make a book.

**Buttons** Mix buttons with beads for extra decorative effect.

**Cord** Beads can be wrapped around a core of three-ply cord, available in many colours from furnishing trimmings suppliers and haberdashery departments.

**Cotton spheres** These are made of compressed cotton fibres and come in various shapes. They are available from specialist trimmings and beading suppliers.

**Cover buttons** Sold in kit form in haberdashery departments, cover buttons consist of two pieces: a top, over which the fabric is pulled, and an underside with shank attached.

**Embroidery threads** These include perlé cotton (a high sheen 2-ply thread), stranded embroidery thread (separate the 5-ply strands for fine work) and machine embroidery threads. They are available in a full range of colours, including metallics.

**Fabric paints** Water-based, non-toxic paints that are fixed by ironing are recommended.

**Fishing twine** For heavy beads, such as glass, fishing twine is recommended. It is stronger than polyester thread but more difficult to work with.

**Floss thread** This fibrous thread has a silk-like sheen.

**Fusible bonding web** Ironed on to the back of appliqué fabric, this bonds it to the ground fabric stitching.

**Interfacing** Normally used to stiffen fabric, it also makes a good ground fabric for beadwork.

**Jewellery findings** Gold- or silver-plated hatpins, earring wires, clasps, brooch backs and other findings are available from beadwork suppliers.

**Lill pins** Shorter than dressmaker's pins, these are ideal for pin-beading.

**Marker pen** This is useful for marking outlines and is also used for drawing decorative patterns.

**Ribbon** Silk, satin and velvet ribbons can all be used to embellish beadwork.

**Tape** Fringes are stitched to fabric tape before being inserted into seams or rolled into tassels.

**Tapestry canvas** This stiff, open-weave canvas is available in various sizes of weave from embroidery suppliers.

**Tapestry wool** This matt wool yarn comes in a wide range of colours.

| | |
|---|---|
| 1 Tapestry wool | 10 Floss thread |
| 2 Cord | 11 Beading wire |
| 3 Beading thread | 12 Jewellery findings |
| 4 Tape | 13 Lill pins |
| 5 Ribbon | 14 Brass screw bindings |
| 6 Fabric paint | 15 Bookbinding fabric |
| 7 Fabric paint | 16 Buttons |
| 8 Cotton spheres | 17 Cover buttons |
| 9 Fishing twine | |

# EQUIPMENT

BEADWORK IS AN IDEAL SMALL-SCALE HOBBY AS IT REQUIRES VERY FEW SPECIALIST TOOLS. BASIC EQUIPMENT SUCH AS SCISSORS, PINS AND RULER WILL PROBABLY ALREADY BE CLOSE TO HAND IN THE SEWING BASKET OR AROUND THE HOME. STORE YOUR BEADS IN SEPARATE GLASS OR PLASTIC CONTAINERS WHERE YOU CAN FIND THEM QUICKLY. WHEN YOU ARE WORKING ON A PROJECT, DECANT THEM INTO SMALL WHITE PALETTES OR SHALLOW SAUCERS.

**Bead loom** This small loom is specially designed for beadwork. The warp threads are fitted between metal springs and wound around wooden rollers. See the supplier information at the back of the book for stockists.

**Beading needles** These fine, long needles are available in various sizes and can be used to thread several beads at a time. They break easily so require careful handling. To thread beads with large holes, you can also use "between" needles.

**Beeswax** This is used to run along the beading thread to increase its strength and prevent it from snagging on sharp edges. It is particularly useful when threading faceted beads.

**Craft knife** A strong knife is needed to cut out card.

**Drawing pins** These are used to pin strands on to a pin board.

**Dressmaker's pins** These are used to pin fabric before tacking or slip stitching.

**Embroidery hoop** Two tightly fitting rings hold fabric taut. Plastic hoops with a metal spring are recommended for use under a sewing machine.

**Embroidery scissors** These small, sharp scissors are used to cut and trim thread and fabric.

**Fabric marker** The marks made with this specialized pen fade on contact with air or water.

**Graph paper** This is used to measure fringes and tassels.

**Metal scissors** Use metal scissors to crack damaged beads and thus remove them from a string.

**Needles** Some dressmaking needles, called "sharps", may be small enough to pass through beads. Leather needles are used to stitch beads to tough material such as leather.

**Paintbrush** This is used to apply fabric paint in some projects.

**Palettes** When working on a project, decant beads into white china palettes, available from artists' suppliers. Alternatively, you can use saucers, as long as you do not mix up the different types of beads.

**Pin board** Fringing or macramé work should be pinned out on a board. It is important that the board is large enough to accommodate the whole design. Small pieces of work can be pinned out on an ironing board.

**Ruler** This is essential for accurate measuring. A metal-edged ruler is the most suitable for these projects.

**Sewing machine** Use the normal foot for straight stitching and the darning foot for machine embroidery.

**Tape measure** Use instead of a ruler for measuring fabric and curved surfaces.

**Tweezers** These are very useful both for selecting and removing individual beads.

**Wire cutters and round-nosed jewellery pliers** These are essential for bending and cutting wire.

1 Pin board
2 Tape measure
3 Ruler
4 Bead loom
5 Sewing machine
6 Palettes
7 Needles
8 Beading needles
9 Paintbrush
10 Fabric marker
11 Pins
12 Embroidery scissors
13 Metal scissors
14 Graph paper
15 Drawing pins
16 Tweezers
17 Embroidery hoop
18 Wire cutters
19 Round-nosed jewellery pliers

# BASIC TECHNIQUES

THE TECHNIQUES USED IN BEADWORK ARE QUITE EASY TO GRASP ONCE YOU UNDERSTAND THE FUNDAMENTAL PRINCIPLES. HOWEVER, WHEN LEARNING ANY NEW SKILL, IT IS WORTH TAKING TIME TO MASTER THE BASICS BEFORE PROGRESSING TO MORE COMPLEX TECHNIQUES. START WITH A QUITE STRAIGHT-FORWARD PROJECT SUCH AS STRINGING BEADS OR MAKING A SHORT FRINGE, THEN PROGRESS TO MORE INTRICATE WORK.

## PRE-STRUNG BEADS

Simply thread a needle and pass it through the beads then remove the old thread.

## BEAD PICOT

Use a tape measure and fabric marker to mark even points. Thread a needle, insert it into the fabric at one end of the picot and secure with a knot. Pass the needle through a large bead, followed by a small bead – the small bead will prevent the large one slipping off. Push both beads as far as possible up the needle then pass the needle back through the large bead. Make a stitch in the fabric to the next marked point.

## LONG FRINGE

1 For an even fringe, use graph paper or count the number of beads and use the same number for each string. Cut a piece of thread four times the length of the fringe desired. Thread both ends through a needle to give a doubled thread. Insert into fabric and secure with a knot. Pass needle through loop in thread and pull taut.

2 Mark the length of the fringe on graph paper and place next to the thread. Thread on the required number of beads, pushing them up as far as possible.

3 Pass the needle through the second to last bead. Check that no thread is visible. Make a fastening-off stitch between the third and fourth beads from the end then continue up the string of beads, making fastening-off stitches every four beads.

4 Pull the string gently to remove kinks in the thread, then trim the thread.

### SHORT FRINGE

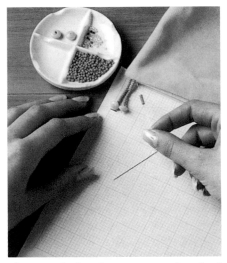

This is worked with a continuous length of thread. Mark the length desired on graph paper. Insert the needle in the fabric and secure the thread with a knot. Thread on the required number of beads, pushing them up as far as possible. Pass the needle through the second to last bead, then back up the full length of the string. Insert the needle back into the fabric and bring it out at the next point on the fringe.

### POINTED FRINGE

Thread a needle, insert in the fabric and secure with a knot. Thread on a bugle bead, a small glass bead and another bugle. Push the beads up as far as possible to form points, then insert the needle at the next point on the fringe.

### DROP FRINGE

Thread a needle, insert in the fabric and secure with a knot. Thread on a small glass bead, a drop bead and another small glass bead. Push the beads up as far as possible, then insert the needle at the next point on the fringe.

## LOOPS

Mark points at even intervals with a fabric marker. Thread a needle, insert into the fabric at the first point and secure with a knot. Thread on enough beads to give the desired size of loop, pushing them up as far as possible. Insert the needle back at the same point to form a loop, then insert the needle at the next point on the fringe.

## LOOPS WITH STEMS

Before making a loop, thread on the required number of beads for the stem, then add the beads for the loop. Pass the needle back through the stem.

## NEEDLE-WOVEN BEADING

In this technique, a continuous thread runs through rounds of beads, with the second round of beads fitting between pairs of the first. The second round is joined to the first by interweaving. The following instructions are for a three-dimensional object. For a two-dimensional design, work rows instead of rounds.

1 For round 1, thread on the required number of beads, tie around the neck of the object and knot the ends.

2 For round 2, pass needle through first bead of round 1, thread first bead of round 2 between first and second beads. Pass needle through third bead of round 1. Continue until design is complete.

## COUCHING

Pre-strung beads are laid down on fabric to create or embellish the lines of the design, then stitched over (couched down) with thread to secure. Add a second thread of beads on top for extra texture.

## SCALLOPS

Mark points at even intervals. Thread a needle, insert it into the fabric at the first point and secure with a knot. Thread on enough beads to give the desired length of scallop, pushing them up as far as possible, then insert the needle back in at the next point.

## THREADING A BEAD LOOM

Bead weaving produces flat, narrow strips of beaded fabric. The beads lie between the warp threads and a continuous weft thread is passed through the beads, over and under the warp threads.

1 Decide the length of the piece required and add 45 cm (18 in). Cut the warp threads to this length. Calculate the number of beads required for the width, depending on the size of bead. Cut one warp thread for each bead, plus one extra. Lay the warp threads out smoothly and tie them together with a knot at each end. Divide the strands evenly into two, then slip one knot over the rivets in the roller. Turn the roller to wind on a little thread, then spread the threads out and arrange them in the spring next to each other.

2 Slip the knot at the other end of the warp over the rivets in the other roller and wind on as before. Adjust the tension by winding the rollers until the warp threads are taut.

3 Thread a beading needle with a long length of thread and draw it through beeswax. Tie the other end of the thread to the far left warp thread 2.5 cm (1 in) from the rollers.

# CHINESE NECKLACE

THE STARTING POINT FOR THIS NECKLACE WAS THE UNUSUAL FILIGREE PENDANT AT THE CENTRE. THE BEADS ARE STRUNG ON A KNOTTED LENGTH. BLANKET STITCH IS WORKED AROUND A CORE OF THREAD, THE STITCHES SPIRALLING AROUND THE THREAD NATURALLY.

**1** For each side cut 2-ply silk thread 1 metre (40 in) long, fold in half and pin midpoint to pin board. Cut two lengths of fine silk 2 metres (80 in) long. Thread each on to a large-eyed needle, double up thread, tie a knot and slip both knots over pin. Lay fine silk thread next to the 2-ply lengths. Work a blanket stitch along the threads for 12 cm (4¼ in).

**2** Separate the 2-ply strands and, using the two needles, work a blanket stitch for 2 cm (1 in) down both lengths.

**3** Thread one bone bead on to one strand and one round amber bead on to the other. Tie double knots just beneath the beads. Continue as for step 1 for another 1.5 cm (⅝ in).

**4** Thread a round lampwork and tie a knot just beneath the bead. Continue as one strand for 1.5 cm (⅝ in), divide in two for 1.5 cm (⅝ in), thread on two precious stone beads, tie knots.

**5** Continue as two strands for 1.5 cm (⅝ in), join strands. Continue as one strand for 1 cm (½ in), thread on lampwork disc, knot, continue as one strand for 1 cm (½ in). Thread on first one bone, then one large amber and another bone bead. Tie a knot. Tie two sides together, thread all ends through pendant and knot.

**6** Thread ends through a lampwork disc and knot. Thread end back through oval bead and trim. Unpin piece, sew clasp to each end.

## MATERIALS AND EQUIPMENT YOU WILL NEED

2-PLY SILK THREAD • SCISSORS • MEASURING TAPE • DRAWING PINS • PIN BOARD • FINE SILK THREAD • 2 LARGE-EYED NEEDLES •
6 BONE BEADS • 2 ROUND AMBER BEADS • 2 ROUND LAMPWORK BEADS WITH FOIL INSERTS • 4 PRECIOUS STONE BEADS • 3 LAMPWORK DISCS WITH
FOIL INSERTS • 2 LARGE AMBER BEADS • 1 LARGE CHINESE PENDANT • 1 CLASP

# VENETIAN NECKLACE

IN THIS SUMPTUOUS CREATION, MULTIPLE STRANDS OF RICHLY COLOURED BEADS ARE JOINED AT INTERVALS WITH LARGE VENETIAN BEADS. THIS IS AN IDEAL WAY TO SHOW OFF A FEW PRECIOUS BEADS BY MIXING THEM WITH A SELECTION OF SMALL INEXPENSIVE BEADS IN TONING COLOURS. CRIMPING BEADS ARE DESIGNED SO THAT THEY CAN BE FIRMLY ATTACHED WITH PLIERS, TO SAFELY CARRY THE FASTENINGS FOR A HEAVY NECKLACE.

1 Cut 250 cm (100 in) of thread and thread through a needle. Tie a bead to the end as an anchor. Thread on the following beads: one lilac, 25 bronze, one green, two bronze, two green, one red, three green, one red, one lilac, one Venetian, one lilac, one red, three green, one red, two green, two bronze, one green. Repeat this sequence six more times. End with 25 bronze and a lilac.

2 Cut another 250 cm (100 in) length of thread, thread through the needle and tie around the anchor bead as before. Pass the needle through the first lilac bead threaded in step 1 then thread on 25 bronze, one green, two bronze, two green, one red and three green. Pass the needle through the red, lilac, Venetian, lilac and red beads threaded in step 1. Repeat this sequence six more times, ending with 25 bronze beads and passing the needle through the lilac bead.

3 Make another three strands the same way. Tie the threads in a tight knot at each end, then attach a brass crimping bead over each knot with pliers.

4 Attach a gold loop to the top of each crimping bead. Thread the fastener through the loops.

## MATERIALS AND EQUIPMENT YOU WILL NEED

SCISSORS • STRONG BLACK NYLON THREAD • NEEDLE • 5MM (1/16 IN) LILAC IRIDESCENT AND RED GLASS BEADS • 3MM BRONZE AND GREEN GLASS BEADS • SEVEN LARGE VENETIAN GLASS BEADS • TWO CRIMPING BEADS WITH LOOPS • ROUND-NOSED JEWELLERY PLIERS • TWO 5MM (1/16 IN) GOLD LOOPS • 1 S-SHAPED GOLD FASTENER

# WRAPPED EARRINGS

THESE RICHLY DECORATIVE EARRINGS ARE SIMPLY MADE OF ROLLED TUBES OF CARD COVERED WITH VELVET RIBBON. THE TUBES ARE THEN WRAPPED WITH METALLIC THREAD AND GOLD WIRE, STUDDED WITH SMALL BEADS; LARGER BEADS ARE ATTACHED WITH HATPINS. RIBBONS AND BEADS ARE BOTH AVAILABLE IN A HUGE RANGE OF COLOURS, SO IT IS EASY TO EXPERIMENT WITH DIFFERENT COLOUR COMBINATIONS TO MATCH A PARTICULAR OUTFIT.

**1** Cut two rectangles of card, each 4 x 7 cm (1½ x 2¾ in). Starting from the short side, roll into narrow tubes 1.5 cm (⅝ in) in diameter.

**2** Cut two pieces of velvet ribbon, 6 cm (2½ in) long. Roll a piece of ribbon around each card tube, right side out.

**3** Fold under the raw edges of the ribbon and slip stitch.

**4** Double red metallic thread, thread on to a needle and knot end. Fasten to end of a tube, wrap evenly around tube and fasten off. Cut 40 pieces of gold wire, 1.5 cm (⅝ in) long. Thread beading thread on to a needle and fasten to a tube. Thread on alternately gold wire and green beads. Wrap around the tube and fasten off.

**5** Push a hatpin through the tube 5 mm (³⁄₁₆ in) from top. Snip ends leaving an equal length each side. Thread a flower bead, large red bead and three small red beads on each side. Twist ends into spiral.

**6** Take a hatpin for each tube, thread on a brass bead, large red bead, hexagonal bead, wrapped tube, then the same beads in reverse. Trim each hatpin end, bend into a loop. Attach earring wires.

## MATERIALS AND EQUIPMENT YOU WILL NEED

THIN CARD • RULER AND PENCIL • SCISSORS • 5 CM (2 IN) WIDE VELVET RIBBON • SEWING NEEDLE •
SEWING THREAD TO MATCH RIBBON • RED METALLIC EMBROIDERY THREAD • TEXTURED GOLD WIRE • WIRE CUTTERS • BEADING NEEDLE •
MATCHING BEADING THREAD • SMALL GREEN GLASS BEADS • FOUR HATPINS • EIGHT 4 MM (³⁄₁₆ IN) FLOWER BRASS BEADS •
EIGHT 6 MM (⁵⁄₁₆ IN) RED GLASS BEADS • TWELVE 4 MM (³⁄₁₆ IN) RED GLASS BEADS • ROUND-NOSED JEWELLERY PLIERS •
FOUR 7 MM (⅜ IN) HEXAGONAL BRASS BEADS • PAIR OF SILVER EARRING WIRES

# BEADED BUTTONS

SIMPLE AND SATISFYING TO MAKE, THESE BEAUTIFUL BUTTONS ADD A UNIQUE FINISHING TOUCH TO A SPECIAL GARMENT OR SOFT FURNISHING PROJECT. THE LUSCIOUS BLACKBERRY BUTTON IS CONSTRUCTED AROUND A COMPRESSED COTTON BALL, AND WOULD LOOK EQUALLY ATTRACTIVE AS A PENDANT HANGING FROM A BRACELET OR NECKLACE. THE OTHER THREE BUTTONS ARE ALL MADE FROM SCRAPS OF SILK AND TAFFETA, USING COVER BUTTON KITS AS A BASE. CHOOSE BETWEEN THICKLY ENCRUSTED BUTTONS COVERED WITH BEADS OR A SIMPLE TASSEL OR FLOWER DESIGN.

1 For the blackberry button: using a black marker pen, cover the cotton sphere completely.

2 Thread the needle and make a few stitches at the top of the sphere to secure. Thread on a small black glass bead, make a stitch then pass the needle right through the sphere. Thread on another bead and stitch down. Take the needle around the sphere, passing through the two beads at top and bottom, then around at right angles to divide it into quarters.

3 Thread on 18 beads and pass the needle through the bottom bead on the sphere. Thread on 18 more beads, pass the needle through the top bead then around the sphere at right angles.

## MATERIALS AND EQUIPMENT YOU WILL NEED

BLACK MARKER PEN • COMPRESSED COTTON SPHERE, 1 CM (½ IN) DIAMETER • NEEDLE AND BLACK THREAD • SMALL BLACK GLASS BEADS •
FABRIC MARKER • 3 CM (1¼ IN) DIAMETER COVER BUTTON • SILK • SCISSORS • THREADS TO MATCH SILK AND TAFFETA•
LARGE TRANSPARENT GLASS BEADS WITH SILVER-LINED HOLES • 4 MM (³⁄₁₆ IN) GREEN CRYSTAL BEADS •1.5 CM (⅝ IN) DIAMETER COVER BUTTONS •
TAFFETA • 5 MM (³⁄₁₆ IN) GREEN GLASS BEAD • SMALL COPPER-COLOURED GLASS BEADS • SMALL TRANSPARENT GLASS BEADS

4 Thread on 16 beads and work from top to bottom as before, this time dividing the sphere into eight sections. Repeat with 14 beads, dividing the sphere into 16 sections, until the whole sphere is covered.

6 For the flower button: using a fabric marker, draw around the 3 cm (1¼ in) cover button on to the silk. Draw another circle 1 cm (⅜ in) larger and cut out. Mark five equally spaced points around the inner circle.

8 Bring the needle out at one of the points marked. Couch down the loop at this point with a stitch between the ninth and tenth beads. Make four more glass-bead petals in the same way.

5 If the blackberry is intended to hang on a bracelet or necklace, fasten on a thread at the bottom and thread on eight beads. Insert the needle back into the sphere at the same point to make a loop.

7 Thread a needle and fasten on in the centre of the circle. Thread on 20 large transparent glass beads, then insert the needle back at the same point to make a loop.

9 Stitch a green crystal bead in the centre of the flower. ▶

**10** Run a gathering stitch 3 mm (⅛ in) from the raw edge. Place the cover button in the centre and pull up the thread. Secure with a few small stitches and attach the underside of the button.

**11** For the tassel button: draw around a 1.5 cm (⅝ in) diameter cover button on to the taffeta, then draw another circle 7 mm (⅜ in) larger and cut out. Thread a needle and fasten on in the centre. Thread on the green glass bead and eight copper beads, then pass the needle back through the green bead and fasten off. Gather the raw edges and attach the cover button as in step 10.

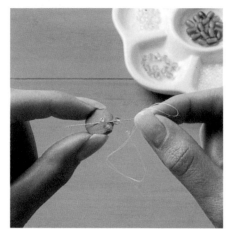

**12** For the jewel-encrusted button: draw around the cover button on to the taffeta, then draw another circle 7 mm (⅜ in) larger and cut out. Run a gathering stitch around the edge and attach the cover button, as in step 10. Thread a needle and fasten on in the centre. Thread on a green crystal bead and some small transparent glass beads, then pass the needle back through the green bead. Make another stitch and repeat until the button is completely covered.

# CORD-BEADED BRACELET

CORD BEADING IS VERY POPULAR AMONGST THE ZULU PEOPLE OF SOUTH AFRICA, WHO ARE SOME OF THE MOST SKILLED AND PROLIFIC BEAD-WORKERS IN THE WORLD. IT IS A VERY SIMPLE TECHNIQUE, IN WHICH THREADS OF SMALL BEADS ARE WOUND AROUND AND THEN STITCHED ON TO A READYMADE CORD CORE. THIS BRACELET HAS A BUTTON AND LOOP FASTENING. TO MAKE A BANGLE, BIND THE ENDS OF THE CORD TOGETHER BEFORE BEADING TO MAKE A CONTINUOUS CIRCLE. FOR A NECKLACE OR BELT, SIMPLY EXTEND THE LENGTH OF THE CORD. YOU CAN VARY THE EFFECT BY MIXING BEADS OF DIFFERENT COLOURS.

1 Bind both ends of the cord tightly with thread. Paint the cord with fabric paint.

2 Thread the needle and fasten to one end of the cord. Thread on 20 beads, holding thread taut and pushing the beads together. Wind the beads around the cord, make a couple of stitches then pass the needle back through the last few beads. Repeat along the length of the cord.

3 To finish the ends of the cord, thread on a few beads and make a stitch across the blunt end. Make several more stitches to completely cover the end.

4 Make a beaded loop at one end of the cord (see Basic Techniques). At the other end, thread on three beads then pass the needle through the button. Thread on two more beads, pass the needle back through the button and make several stitches to finish off.

MATERIALS AND EQUIPMENT YOU WILL NEED

THICK CORD • THREAD • FABRIC PAINT, TO MATCH BEADS • PAINTBRUSH • BEADING NEEDLE • BEADING THREAD • SMALL GLASS BEADS • BUTTON, DIAMETER TO MATCH CORD

# SEQUINNED CHRISTMAS DECORATIONS

SEQUINS MAKE WONDERFUL CHRISTMAS DECORATIONS, TWINKLING AND SPARKLING AS THEY CATCH THE LIGHT. USE CONCAVE SEQUINS RATHER THAN FLAT ONES AS THEY WILL GIVE THE FINISHED BAUBLES A SMOOTH SURFACE. LILL PINS ARE USED TO HOLD THE SEQUINS IN PLACE – BECAUSE THEY ARE SHORTER THAN DRESSMAKER'S PINS, THEY WILL NOT CLOG THE COTTON SPHERE FOUNDATION. THE PINS ALSO GIVE THE BAUBLES A PLEASING WEIGHT.

**1** Using a marker pen, divide the surface of the cotton sphere into quarters, as shown. Mark around the middle of the sphere to divide it into eight sections.

**3** Fill in the sections, again overlapping the sequins slightly.

**5** To make the star bauble, mark several horizontal stripes. Press in a sequin at the top and bottom. Working outwards from these points, press in silver pointed sequins to form a star shape.

**2** Outline the sections with round concave sequins, using different colours. Use lill pins to attach the sequins and overlap them slightly.

**4** Using a beading needle and thread, make several small stitches in the top of the sphere. Thread on 8 cm (3 in) of small bronze glass beads then make several more stitches, to make a loop for hanging. Thread a metal bead on to a pin and press into the sphere to secure the loop.

**6** Fill in the rest of sphere with round sequins, as in steps 2 and 3. As an alternative hanging loop, attach a 10 cm (4 in) piece of ribbon to the top, using a dressmaker's pin and metal bead as in step 4.

## MATERIALS AND EQUIPMENT YOU WILL NEED

TWO COMPRESSED COTTON SPHERES, 6 CM (2½ IN) DIAMETER • MARKER PEN • 5 MM (³⁄₁₆ IN) DIAMETER ROUND CONCAVE SEQUINS IN A VARIETY OF COLOURS, INCLUDING METALLIC • LILL PINS • BEADING NEEDLE • BEADING THREAD • SMALL BRONZE-COLOURED GLASS BEADS • FLUTED METAL BEADS • DRESSMAKER'S PINS • SILVER POINTED OVAL SEQUINS • RIBBON

# DEVORÉ SCARF

THE LEAF PATTERN ON THIS DEVORÉ VELVET FABRIC IS ECHOED IN APPLIQUÉ AND BEADWORK. SOME LEAF SHAPES ARE CUT OUT OF THE DEVORÉ FABRIC AND FUSED TO THE ORGANZA BACKING, OTHERS ARE STITCHED WITH TINY SEQUINS AND EMBROIDERY THREAD. TO COMPLETE THE EFFECT, BEADED FLOWERS ARE DOTTED AMONGST THE LEAVES. THE SCARF IS FINISHED WITH A DRAMATIC SILK BINDING IN A CONTRASTING COLOUR.

1 Cut a square of devoré velvet 20 x 20 cm (8 x 8 in). Using a hot iron, fuse the bonding web to the wrong side. Cut out individual leaf shapes from the fabric using embroidery scissors.

2 Peel away the backing paper from the leaf shapes. Scatter them on one end of the organza, right sides up, and fuse in place with a hot iron.

3 Attach a darning foot to the sewing machine and set to darning mode. Place the organza in an embroidery hoop and zigzag stitch around the edge of each leaf in matching thread. ▶

## MATERIALS AND EQUIPMENT YOU WILL NEED

SCISSORS • 28 CM (11 IN) OF 130 CM (52 IN) WIDE DEVORÉ VELVET, WITH LEAF PATTERN • IRON • FUSIBLE BONDING WEB • EMBROIDERY SCISSORS • 20 CM (8 IN) OF 110 CM (45 IN) WIDE ORGANZA • SEWING MACHINE AND DARNING FOOT • MATCHING SEWING THREADS • EMBROIDERY HOOP • FABRIC MARKER • NEEDLE • MATCHING EMBROIDERY THREAD • SMALL SILVER SEQUINS • SMALL SILVER GLASS BEADS • 5 MM (³⁄₁₆ IN) BLUE OVAL BEADS • 10 CM (4 IN) OF 110 CM (45 IN) WIDE SILK, IN CONTRASTING COLOUR

4 Using a fabric marker, draw extra leaves scattered over the scarf.

6 Fill in a few of the drawn shapes with small silver beads applied by hand. To make the flowers, stitch a small silver bead in the centre of a sequin. Bring the needle out on one side of the sequin, then thread on a silver bead, a blue bead and another silver. Insert the needle in the fabric and bring out on the other side of the sequin. Stitch five more petals around the sequin.

7 Cut a piece of devoré fabric 28 x 110 cm (11 x 45 in). Wrong sides together, machine stitch to the organza on all four sides. Cut strips of contrasting silk fabric 3 cm (1¼ in) wide, stitch together and press to make a continuous binding. Right sides together, stitch all around the scarf. Fold the binding over the edge of the scarf, tuck under the raw edges and slip stitch.

5 Place the end with the devoré leaves in the embroidery hoop. To fill in the drawn shapes, fasten on sequins with matching embroidery thread. Thread on a sequin, then make a stitch at the side of it. Bring the needle up on the other side, thread on another sequin, then insert the needle in the centre of the first sequin. Bring it out on the other side of the second sequin. Overlap the sequins to lie smoothly.

*Above: Devoré velvet never dates and has a subtle elegance that is very flattering.*

# WOVEN BRACELET

INSPIRED BY THE DESIGNS OF THE ART DECO MOVEMENT, THE DESIGNER HAS CHOSEN PEARLIZED ICE-CREAM COLOURS IN A GEOMETRIC PATTERN. THE PIECE IS WORKED IN SMALL GLASS BEADS ON A BEAD LOOM. AS WHEN WEAVING FABRICS, THE WARP THREADS (VERTICAL THREADS) ARE STRETCHED TAUT, WHILE THE WEFT THREADS (HORIZONTAL THREADS) PASS BACKWARDS AND FORWARDS UNDER AND OVER THE WARP. LONG NARROW BRAIDS CAN BE PRODUCED WITH THESE LOOMS.

1 Measure the diameter of your wrist to determine the length of your bracelet and add an extra 45 cm (18 in). Cut 21 warp threads to the total length. Lay out the threads and knot together at each end. Divide evenly into two strands. Slip one knot over the roller rivets. Wind on a little thread by turning the roller, then spread the threads out and arrange them in the spring next to each other.

2 Slip the knot at the other end of the warp over the rivets in the other roller and wind on. Wind the rollers on to adjust the tension – the warp threads should be taut.

3 Thread a beading needle with a long thread and draw the thread through beeswax. Tie the other end of the thread to the far left warp thread 2.5 cm (1 in) from the rollers. ▶

## MATERIALS AND EQUIPMENT YOU WILL NEED

BEAD LOOM • BEADING THREAD • SCISSORS • BEADING NEEDLE • BEESWAX • SMALL LIGHT GREEN, PINK, GREY AND PURPLE GLASS BEADS • STICKY TAPE • WOOL LINING FABRIC • SEWING NEEDLE • THREAD • 3 BUTTONS WITH SHANKS

4 Following the pattern in the template section at the back of the book, thread on 20 beads. Push them up as far as they will go, fitting them in place between the warp threads. With the forefinger push the beads through the spaces, passing the needle back through the beads in the opposite direction above the warp thread. Pull the thread tight. Thread on 20 more beads and continue along the warp in the same way.

5 To finish off, pass the needle back through several rows of beads, tie a knot and trim the thread.

7 Cut a piece of wool lining fabric to the same size as the finished work. Tuck the free warp edges under and assemble the work and the lining wrong sides together. Work a slip stitch all around the finished piece.

6 To remove the work from the loom, cut 2 pieces of sticky tape and stick in place over the warp threads at either end of the work. Cut the threads.

8 On one end of the bracelet, stitch 3 buttons at equal distances, on the other end make 3 beaded loops large enough to fit over the buttons.

# WALLET

THE BIRD MOTIF ON THIS ATTRACTIVE WALLET IS MADE FROM BLUE SILK EMBELLISHED WITH SATIN AND RUNNING STITCH. INTERESTING FRAGMENTS OF DRIFTWOOD PROVIDE SOME TEXTURAL CONTRAST AND WORK EXTREMELY WELL WITH THE OVERALL THEME. GOLD CORD, METALLIC EMBROIDERY THREADS AND A SELECTION OF BEADS HELP TO CREATE AN OBJET D'ART THAT, WHEN FINISHED, WILL LOOK AS VALUABLE AS ITS CONTENTS.

1 Trace the bird design from the back of the book and make a card template. For the top side cut a piece of silk 45 cm x 15 cm (18 in x 6 in). Fold the fabric in thirds lengthways and draw around the template. Cut pieces of drift-wood and arrange them across the bird shape. Using matching thread, couch the wood in place.

2 Cut a length of gold cord and wind back and forth across shape, couching it in place with red embroidery thread. Stitch small red beads and other beads to the design. Work a satin stitch for the beak and a running stitch around the shape.

3 For the underside, cut a silk piece 45 cm x 15 cm (18 in x 6 in). To stiffen wallet, cut a piece of heavyweight interfacing 45 cm x 15 cm (18 in x 6 in). Cut 2 pieces of fusible bonding web to the same size. Fuse in place on either side of the interfacing with a hot iron. Remove the paper back. Fold the piece into thirds lengthways. Fuse underside piece in place.

4 Turn the work over and fuse the top-side piece, carefully ironing around the embroidered and beaded area. For the pocket, cut two pieces each of silk and fusible bonding web and one of interfacing 15 cm x 15 cm (6 in x 6 in) and bond together as before. Place the pocket at one end of the wallet on the underside and pin. Work a decorative zigzag stitch all around the edge.

MATERIALS AND EQUIPMENT YOU WILL NEED
PENCIL • CARD • SCISSORS • TAPE MEASURE • BLUE DUPION SILK APPROX 50 CM X 50 CM (20 IN X 20 IN) • FABRIC MARKER • SMALL PIECES OF DRIFTWOOD • CRAFT KNIFE • NEEDLE • THICK COTTON THREAD • GOLD CORD • EMBROIDERY NEEDLE • RED, PURPLE AND SILVER METALLIC EMBROIDERY THREAD • SMALL RED GLASS BEADS • RED BEAD • SILVER BEAD • LONG GOLD BEADS • HEART BEAD • BRASS BEAD • HEAVYWEIGHT INTERFACING • FUSIBLE BONDING WEB • IRON • PINS • SEWING MACHINE AND MATCHING THREADS

# DRAMATIC PAINTED GLOVES

THESE GLOVES ARE PAINTED WITH VIBRANT RED SHOE DYE AND THEN A FREE-HAND DESIGN IS PICKED OUT WITH TINY BEADS. THE BEADS ARE SEWN ON INDIVIDUALLY SO THIS IS A VERY EASY FIRST PROJECT FOR A BEGINNER. YOU NEED A STRONG, SHARP NEEDLE TO STITCH THROUGH THE LEATHER; ALTERNATIVELY, YOU CAN USE FABRIC GLOVES. DO NOT EXTEND THE DESIGN TOO FAR DOWN THE GLOVE AS IT WILL BE DIFFICULT TO SEW.

1 Put each glove on to prevent it from shrinking. Paint on the red dye and leave to dry.

3 Thread the needle with nylon filament. Stitch green beads individually in a row along the cuff edge of each glove.

5 Stitch individual red glass beads at random intervals over the back of the gloves as shown.

2 Draw an abstract design freehand on the back of each glove, using a fabric marker. Start from the cuff end.

4 Stitch more green beads along the lines of the design.

6 Outline the remainder of the design with gold beads. Fill in the shapes with pink beads.

## MATERIALS AND EQUIPMENT YOU WILL NEED

LIGHTWEIGHT LEATHER GLOVES • RED LEATHER SHOE DYE • PAINTBRUSH • FABRIC MARKER • FINE LEATHER NEEDLE • NYLON FILAMENT •
SMALL GREEN, RED, GOLD AND PINK GLASS BEADS

# PEARL TIARA

THIS PRETTY TIARA IS HEAVILY ENCRUSTED WITH SPIRALS OF ARTIFICIAL PEARLS TO MAKE A SCALLOPED EDGING. THE DESIGNER HAS COUCHED DIFFERENT SIZED BEADS ON TO A BACKING STIFFENED WITH WIRE WHICH MAY BE STITCHED TO A USEFUL COMB OR HAIR CLIP. IT WOULD BE AN IDEAL HAIR ADORNMENT FOR A BRIDE TO HOLD A VEIL IN PLACE. FOR BRIDESMAIDS, CHOOSE FROM A WIDE RANGE OF PEARLIZED COLOURS INSTEAD OF IVORY.

1 Trace the template from the back of the book on to card and cut out. Mark around the template twice on the heavyweight interfacing and cut out.

2 Bend a loop at each end of the millinery wire. Stitch the wire to one piece of the interfacing 2 cm (¾ in) from the straight edge.

3 Following the template guide, mark the centre of each scallop on the right side of the wire-stiffened interfacing. Stitch the largest bead of 1 cm (½ in) to the centre of the middle scallop. Bring the needle through to the right side next to the last bead and thread on approximately eight 6 mm (¼ in) beads and enough 4 mm (⅕ in) beads to spiral outwards to fill the scallop shape, then make a fastening stitch to secure.

4 Thread a sewing needle with matching thread and make tiny stitches over the beading thread in between the pearl beads. Repeat for the other scallops using 8 mm (⅖ in) beads in the centre of each. Couch down the small beads to fill in the remaining interfacing.

5 Stitch the back piece of the tiara to the front with slip stitch. Stitch the drop beads between the scallops.

6 Stitch the comb on the wrong side to the bottom edge of the beaded piece.

## MATERIALS AND EQUIPMENT YOU WILL NEED

CARD • PENCIL • CRAFT KNIFE • HEAVYWEIGHT INTERFACING • FABRIC MARKER • EMBROIDERY SCISSORS • 17.5 CM (7 IN) MILLINERY WIRE • JEWELLERY PLIERS • SEWING NEEDLE • MATCHING THREAD • BEADING NEEDLE • MATCHING BEADING THREAD • ONE LARGE PEARL BEAD, 1 CM (½ IN) • MEDIUM-SIZED PEARLS, 6 MM (¼ IN) • SMALL PEARLS, 4 MM (⅕ IN) • FOUR LARGE PEARL BEADS, 8 MM (⅖ IN) • DROP BEADS • PLASTIC HAIR COMB

# BEAD-TRIMMED CUSHIONS

THE SIMPLEST CUSHION CAN BE DRAMATICALLY TRANSFORMED WITH A BEAD-WORK EDGING. THESE THREE DESIGNS SHOW HOW BEADS OF DIFFERENT WEIGHTS AND SIZES GIVE DIFFERENT EFFECTS. SMALL BEADS MAKE A BEAUTIFULLY DELICATE FRINGE, WHILE LARGE GLASS BEADS GIVE A MUCH FIRMER, BOLD EDGING. CHOOSE BEADS TO CONTRAST OR TO BLEND SUBTLY WITH THE FABRIC. MEASURE THE SIZE OF CUSHION PAD REQUIRED AND ALLOW EXTRA FABRIC FOR THE COVER.

1 For the yellow cushion with bead border: to make the the front cover, cut one piece of velvet the size of the cushion pad plus 2 cm (¾ in) seam allowance all around. For the back cover, cut two pieces of velvet the same width and two-thirds the length. Press under a double hem on both short sides of the back cover and machine stitch. With right sides facing and the stitched edges overlapping, pin the front and back covers together. Machine stitch all around. Turn right side out.

2 Thread beading needle with doubled sewing thread. Make several fastening-on stitches in the seam at one corner. Working from left to right, thread on two white glass beads, one yellow bead and one copper bead. Pass the needle back through the yellow bead and thread on two white glass beads. Insert the needle into the seam 2 cm (¾ in) to the right.

3 Make a tiny stitch, then thread on a blue or white opaque bead and a copper bead. Pass the needle back through the blue or white bead, then insert the needle 2 cm (¾ in) further on. Repeat the sequence all around the cover.

## MATERIALS AND EQUIPMENT YOU WILL NEED

TAPE MEASURE • SQUARE CUSHION PAD • SCISSORS • YELLOW VELVET • IRON • SEWING MACHINE AND MATCHING THREAD • DRESSMAKER'S PINS • BEADING NEEDLE • MATCHING THREAD • 5 MM (⅟₁₆ IN) WHITE GLASS BEADS • 7 MM (⅜ IN) OPAQUE YELLOW BEADS • SMALL COPPER-COLOURED GLASS BEADS • 7 MM (⅜ IN) OPAQUE WHITE BEADS • 7 MM (⅜ IN) OPAQUE BLUE BEADS • RECTANGULAR CUSHION PAD • STRIPED FABRIC • FABRIC MARKER • GRAPH PAPER • PENCIL • SMALL PINK AND YELLOW GLASS BEADS • 7 MM (⅜ IN) YELLOW DISC-SHAPED BEADS • RECTANGULAR CUSHION PAD • PINK VELVET • SMALL YELLOW AND PINK GLASS BEADS • 5 MM (⅟₁₆ IN) WHITE GLASS BEADS • 5 MM (⅟₁₆ IN) TURQUOISE GLASS BEADS

4 For the striped cushion with fringe: to make the front cover, cut a piece of fabric the size of the cushion pad plus 2 cm (¾ in) on the width and 20 cm (8 in) on the length. For the back, cut two pieces the same width as the front and two-thirds the length. Press under a double hem on the short back opening edges and machine stitch. With right sides facing and stitched edges overlapping, pin and stitch length-ways seam. Turn right side out and press. Mark a line 10 cm (4 in) from raw edges on both sides and top stitch. Carefully pull away the fabric close to the stitching. Starting from the outer edges, separate and remove threads up to the line.

5 Mark the desired length of fringe 10 cm (4 in) on graph paper. Cut thread four times this measurement and double through the needle. Insert the needle at the inner edge of the first stripe of the fabric and secure with a knot, pass needle through the loop and pull taut.

7 For the pink lattice-trimmed cushion: make up the velvet cover as in step 1. Mark points 1.5 cm (⅝ in) apart along two opposite sides.

6 Mix a few pink with the yellow beads. Thread on 9.5 cm (3¾ in) of beads, using graph paper as a guide. Thread on a disc and a small yellow bead. Pass the needle back through the disc, make a finishing stitch, pass needle up the strand and make another finishing stitch. Pull gently on the strand to iron out kinks. Trim thread. Repeat with the other stripes.

8 Repeat this sequence along the length of the cushion. Fasten on into the seam at one corner with several tiny stitches. Mix a few yellow with the pink beads, thread on 2 cm (¾ in). Add one white bead, 2 cm (¾ in) of pink or yellow and one turquoise and one copper bead. Using the copper bead as an anchor, pass needle back through turquoise bead, thread on 2 cm (¾ in) pink or yellow, a large white, then more pink or yellow. Insert needle into velvet at the third marked point.

►

**9** Make a back stitch to bring the needle out at the second marked point. Thread on 2 cm (¾ in) of pink or yellow beads, then pass the needle through the white bead already in place.

**10** Thread on another 2 cm (¾ in) of pink or yellow beads, one turquoise and one copper bead. Repeat the lattice sequence along each side of the cushion.

# VELVET BOLSTER CUSHION

To make firm edgings and fringes, wire adds body to even the finest beadwork and is therefore ideal for furnishing projects. In this dramatic bolster, small glass beads in a strongly contrasting colour are threaded on to wire and then into the velvet fabric to create three-dimensional curling tendrils. The fine beading wire acts in the same way as a needle and thread to "stitch" through the fabric.

1 Measure the diameter of the end of the bolster cushion and divide in half to find the radius. Draw a circle to this size on paper, using a pair of compasses, then redraw, adding a 1.5 cm (⅝ in) seam allowance. Cut two circles in velvet.

2 Measure the length and circumference of the bolster. Cut a piece of embossed velvet to this size plus 3 cm (1¼ in) seam allowance all round.

3 Tie one end of a piece of beading wire in a knot and pass through the centre of a velvet circle to the right side. Thread on red beads for 10 cm (4 in). Insert the end of the wire back into the velvet 4 cm (1¼ in) from the knot to make a loop. ▶

MATERIALS AND EQUIPMENT YOU WILL NEED

Bolster cushion pad • Tape measure • Pair of compasses • Pencil and paper • Scissors • 50 cm (20 in) of 1 m (39 in) wide blue-black embossed velvet • 0.2 mm beading wire • Small red glass beads • Sewing needle • Matching thread • Sewing machine and matching threads • Dressmaker's pins

4 Thread the wire through the fabric again 5 cm (2 in) from the first loop. Make a second loop as before. Repeat until there are about 20 loops, using extra wire as needed. Fasten the wire off securely. Repeat for the second circle.

5 Run a gathering stitch round each circle, using matching sewing thread.

6 With right sides together, fold the large piece of embossed velvet in half lengthways. Machine stitch the long edge, leaving a 1.5 cm (⅝ in) seam. Leave a gap large enough to insert the cushion pad.

7 Insert the cushion pad and pin and slip stitch the gap.

*Above: The finished bolster cushion feels as luxurious as it looks.*

# DRAWSTRING BAG

INSPIRED BY ETHNIC BEADWORK, THIS ATTRACTIVE LITTLE BAG IS MADE OF TRADITIONAL IKAT FABRIC FROM INDONESIA, LINED WITH A CONTRASTING PLAIN FABRIC. THE LINING ALSO ACTS AS A BINDING AND CASING FOR THE SHOELACE DRAWSTRING TIES. THE BAG IS QUILTED WITH RUNNING STITCH THEN DECORATED WITH A POINTED BEADWORK FRINGE WHICH ECHOES THE DIAGONAL PATTERN OF THE STITCHING. THIS IS AN IDEAL FIRST PROJECT FOR A NEWCOMER TO BEADWORK.

**1** Cut the ikat fabric into two pieces 15 cm (6 in) square. On the right side of each piece, mark a line diagonally from corner to corner in both directions, then mark parallel lines 2 cm (¾ in) apart.

**2** Trace a bag shape similar to the bag in the finished picture and transfer on to card. Lay the card template on both pieces of ikat fabric and cut out. Cut two pieces of plain fabric 16 x 20 cm (6¼ x 8 in) for the lining. With the marked lines right side up, tack one bag piece to each lining piece. Using running stitch, stitch along the lines. Trim the excess lining fabric.

**3** To make the casing, cut two pieces of lining fabric 7 x 12 cm (2¾ x 4¾ in). Press in half lengthways then press in a 1 cm (½ in) turning all round. Pin one long edge to the top of the bag as shown and machine stitch. Repeat with the second casing. ▶

MATERIALS AND EQUIPMENT YOU WILL NEED

SCISSORS • 30 x 15 CM (12 x 6 IN) IKAT FABRIC • SET SQUARE OR RULER • FABRIC MARKER • PENCIL AND PAPER •
THIN CARD • 35 x 35 CM (14 x 14 IN) PLAIN-COLOURED FABRIC, IN CONTRASTING COLOUR • IRON • DRESSMAKER'S PINS •
SEWING MACHINE AND MATCHING THREAD • NEEDLE AND THREAD TO MATCH LINING • BEADING NEEDLE • BLACK STRANDED EMBROIDERY THREAD •
SMALL BLACK GLASS BEADS • SMALL MULTICOLOURED GLASS BEADS • TWO 50 CM (20 IN) BLACK SHOELACES • 12 LARGE BEADS WITH LARGE HOLES

4 Place the two bag pieces right sides together. Pin, then machine stitch 1 cm (½ in) from the raw edges. Leave the top open.

5 Turn the bag right side out. Fold the casings over the raw edges and slip stitch in place.

6 Thread a beading needle with stranded embroidery thread and fasten on at one end of the machine-stitched seamline. Thread on seven black beads and one coloured bead, then pass the needle back through the last black bead. Thread on six more black beads and make a small stitch along the seamline 1 cm (½ in) to the side. Repeat all around the seamline.

7 Thread one shoelace through each casing for the drawstring. Thread three large beads on to the end of each shoelace and knot. Tie the two shoelaces together at either end.

# CHILD'S SLIPPERS

A TINY PAIR OF CHILD'S SLIPPERS ARE EMBROIDERED WITH A GOLDEN STREAM OF BUGLE BEADS. INSTEAD OF STITCHING THE BEADS INDIVIDUALLY, A STRING OF BUGLE BEADS IS LAID ACROSS EACH SLIPPER AND A SECOND THREAD STITCHED OVER IT TO COUCH DOWN THE BEADS. THE TEMPLATES AT THE BACK OF THE BOOK ARE FOR THE LEFT SLIPPER; REVERSE THEM FOR THE RIGHT SLIPPER. FOR LARGER SIZES, YOU CAN SCALE UP THE TEMPLATES ON A PHOTOCOPIER.

1 Enlarge the templates from the back of the book to the size required. For each slipper, cut four back pieces from blue wool. Stitch the back seams together, then assemble each pair, wrong sides together. Work a zigzag stitch along top and bottom edges. Using a sewing machine with a darning foot, stitch wavy lines over the pieces to quilt.

2 To make bias binding fold a velvet square in half diagonally, unfold and mark the line. Mark parallel lines across the cloth 3 cm (1¼ in) apart. Cut along the lines. Match the raw edges of bias binding to the top edge of the back piece. Stitch the binding 6 mm (¼ in) from the edge of the slipper, fold binding over and tuck under raw edges. Slip stitch in place.

3 Cut one piece of fabric to the size of the template for the toe piece. Stitch the dart. Cut out the piece for the beaded appliqué, pin it to the toe as shown. Work a zigzag stitch around the appliqué.

4 Stitch 30 cm (12 in) of bias binding to top edge of the toe piece, by folding the binding in half widthways and pinning. Pin the fold to the centre of the front edge of the toe piece, right sides facing. Pin all around the front edge and stitch 6mm (¼ in) from raw edges. ▶

MATERIALS AND EQUIPMENT YOU WILL NEED

PAPER AND PENCIL • SCISSORS • 50 x 50 CM (20 x 20 IN) PALE BLUE WOOL FABRIC • SEWING MACHINE AND DARNING FOOT • MATCHING SEWING THREADS • 30 x 30 CM (12 x 12 IN) DARK GREY VELVET • FABRIC MARKER • SEWING NEEDLE AND MATCHING THREAD • DRESSMAKER'S PINS • BEADING NEEDLE • BEADING THREAD • GOLD BUGLE BEADS • 20 x 20 CM (8 x 8 IN) GREY WOOL FABRIC • 20 x 20 CM (8 x 8 IN) WADDING

5 At the top edge of the appliquéd piece, make a few fastening-on stitches, then thread on enough bugle beads to follow the line of the piece and insert the beading needle at the other side.

7 Completely cover the appliquéd piece with rows of couching that follow the contours of the first row of beads.

9 Match the centre back to the centre heel of the sole and pin the back piece round the sole. Pin and machine stitch 6 mm (¼ in) from the edge. Pin the toe piece in place over the front, and machine stitch. Stitch the sides of the toe piece to the back where they meet. Pin the bias binding round the base of the back of the slipper, turn both ends under at the centre back and slip stitch the join. Fold the bias binding over the edge of the sole, and slip stitch in place on the underside.

6 Thread up a second needle, make tiny stitches over the laid thread between the first and second bead, push the third bead up close and make another couching stitch between that and the fourth bead.

8 For each slipper, cut two pieces of grey wool fabric and one of wadding to the size of the template. Assemble the wadding between the wool pieces. Set the sewing machine to darning mode and attach a darning foot then stitch a wavy line to quilt the layers. Work a wide zig-zag stitch round the edge.

# BOTTLE COLLAR

This exquisite decoration is made by needle-woven beading (see Basic Techniques). It creates an openwork structure similar to lace but, although the result looks intricate, the technique is very simple. Using a needle and thread, each round of beads is woven into the previous round, with the second round fitting between pairs of the first. The number of beads in each round increases so that the collar expands to cover the top of the bottle with a honeycomb net of beads. The combination of red, green, purple and silver would look great at Christmas.

1 Begin by threading an even number of light green beads on to a long length of thread. This gives you round 1 of the collar. Tie around the neck of the bottle and tie knots at the ends.

2 For round 2, pass the needle through the first bead of round 1, add a red bead then pass it through alternate light green beads. Continue to thread a red bead between each pair of green beads. Pass the needle through the first red bead of this round to begin round 3.

3 For round 3, thread a light green bead between each pair of red beads. Pass the needle through the first light green bead of this round to begin round 4.

4 For round 4, thread an oval bead, a light green bead and another oval bead, then pass the needle through the second light green bead of round 3 to create loops. ▶

MATERIALS AND EQUIPMENT YOU WILL NEED
BEADING NEEDLE • BEADING THREAD • 4 MM (³⁄₁₆ IN) LIGHT GREEN ROUND GLASS BEADS • GLASS BOTTLE, WITH CORK STOPPER •
5 MM (³⁄₁₆ IN) RED DIAMOND GLASS BEADS • 5 MM (³⁄₁₆ IN) BRIGHT GREEN OVAL GLASS BEADS • SMALL PURPLE GLASS BEADS • SMALL SILVER BEADS •
EIGHT LARGE DROP BEADS WITH SILVER FOIL INSERTS • SCISSORS • LILL PINS

5 For round 5, thread the following beads: three purple, one light green, one red, one light green, six purple, one light green, one red, one silver. Pass the needle back through the red and light green beads then thread on seven purple, one light green, one red, one light green and three purple beads.

6 Pass the needle through the third light green bead of round 4. Repeat in sequence all round the collar. Pass the needle through the first light green bead of the round then through an oval bead, a light green bead and another oval bead. Pass the needle through the second light green bead to begin the sequence again.

7 For round 6, thread on three purple beads and one light green bead through red beads of round 5. Add one light green, nine purple, one light green, one large drop, one red and one silver bead. Pass needle back through preceding three beads: red, drop and light green. Thread on nine purple beads and one light green then pass needle through the red bead of round 5. Thread on one light green and three purple beads then pass needle through fourth light green bead of round 4. Repeat the sequence. Pull up thread tightly and fasten off. Pass needle through several beads and snip the thread.

8 Thread a silver bead and a red bead on each lill pin then press them into the cork at an angle so that they fan out at the edge. Pin a silver bead and a large drop into the centre of the cork stopper.

# BEAD CANDLE-HOLDER

TO MAKE A THREE-DIMENSIONAL OBJECT, BEADS ARE THREADED ON TO WIRE AND WOUND AROUND A FRAME WHICH IS CONSTRUCTED OVER A SOLID FORM AND REMOVED AT THE END. BOWLS CAN ALSO BE MADE IN THE SAME WAY.

INEXPENSIVE GLASS BEADS LOOK VERY EFFECTIVE IN THIS STYLISH MODERN DESIGN. THE RESTRAINED SHADES OF GREY, WHITE AND GOLD COME TO LIFE IN THE GLOW OF CANDLELIGHT. A LARGE NIGHTLIGHT WILL FIT COMFORTABLY INSIDE THE FRAME.

1 Cut two pieces of 0.6 mm wire twice the height and diameter of the glass plus 10 cm (4 in). Twist the wires together at their halfway points, then tape the knot to the centre of the glass base. Slip an elastic band over the glass to hold the wire in place. Fold ends over lip of the glass.

2 Cut two pieces of 0.2 mm wire approximately 1 m (39 in) long. Find their halfway points, then twist both pieces around the knot on the base of the glass. Wrap each wire around your hand to prevent it from becoming entangled.

3 Thread the grey glass beads on to the 0.6 mm gold wire.

4 To begin the winding wire, use the pliers to wind one end of the remainder of the thicker wire into a flat spiral 2 cm (¾ in) across. Secure at the centre of the base by weaving the thinner wire over and under the frame and the spiralled wire.

5 Thread more grey beads on to winding wire and continue to wind it into a spiral, weaving the thinner wire under and over frame. Continue up the sides of the glass to within 1 cm (½ in) of the top.

6 Remove elastic. To make a lip, ease top of the frame outwards and thread on white beads. Continue to weave the thinner wire under and over the winding wire and the frame. Thread on small gold beads. Open out ends of frame, remove glass, trim ends and fold back over. Using thinner wire secure the ends to frame.

MATERIALS AND EQUIPMENT YOU WILL NEED

WIRE CUTTERS • 0.6 MM GOLD WIRE • GLASS TUMBLER • ADHESIVE TAPE • LARGE ELASTIC BAND • 0.2 MM GOLD WIRE • ROUND-NOSED JEWELLERY PLIERS • 4MM (³⁄₁₆ IN) GREY GLASS BEADS • 4MM (³⁄₁₆ IN) WHITE GLASS BEADS • 4MM (³⁄₁₆ IN) GOLD-COLOURED GLASS BEADS

# MILK JUG COVER

BRODERIE ANGLAISE AND BEADS ARE A TRADITIONAL COMBINATION, THE BEADS ENHANCING THE DELICATE PATTERN OF THE EDGING. THE HEAVY GLASS BEADS ALSO PROVIDE THE WEIGHT THE MUSLIN COVER NEEDS TO HANG WELL. YOU CAN MAKE A LARGER COVER FOR SUMMER ENTERTAINING WITH JUGS OF HOME-MADE LEMONADE OR CIDER. THE SAME IDEA WOULD ALSO LOOK VERY PRETTY USED TO WEIGHT MUSLIN CURTAINS OR AS A SHELF EDGING.

1 Draw around the saucer on to the muslin. Cut out, leaving an extra 1.5 cm (⅝ in) hem allowance all around. Turn under a single hem and tack.

2 Run a gathering stitch along the top edge of the broderie anglaise and draw up to fit the muslin. Slip stitch the broderie anglaise on to the muslin hem, turning under the raw edges and stitching them together. Trim excess muslin hem.

3 Thread the needle with beading thread. Stitch a row of alternate pale and dark green beads around the edge of the muslin.

4 Fasten the thread on at the point of a scallop in the broderie anglaise. Thread two pink beads, one green heart, one pink, two dark green beads, three pale green, five white, one Venetian, five white, three pale green, two dark green, one pink, one green heart and two pink.

5 Insert the needle at another scallop point, then pass the needle back through the last two pink beads and green heart to make a loop. Continue this sequence all around the edge. Picking out the delicate patterns in the broderie anglaise, stitch tiny flowers. Stitch two rows of four pink beads next to each other with a dark green bead in the centre.

MATERIALS AND EQUIPMENT YOU WILL NEED

FABRIC MARKER • SMALL SAUCER • APPROXIMATELY 20 x 20 CM (8 x 8 IN) MUSLIN, TO FIT SAUCER • SCISSORS • FINE NEEDLE • MATCHING THREADS • 50 CM (20 IN) NARROW BRODERIE ANGLAISE • BEADING THREAD • SMALL 2MM (¹⁄₁₆ IN) GLASS BEADS: PALE GREEN, DARK GREEN, WHITE AND PINK • GREEN HEART-SHAPED BEADS • 5 MM (³⁄₁₆ IN) WHITE VENETIAN BEADS

# NEEDLEPOINT PHOTOGRAPH ALBUM

Hᴇʀᴇ ᴀ ᴛʀᴀᴅɪᴛɪᴏɴᴀʟ Vɪᴄᴛᴏʀɪᴀɴ ᴄʀᴀꜰᴛ ʜᴀs ʙᴇᴇɴ ʙʀᴏᴜɢʜᴛ ᴜᴘ ᴛᴏ ᴅᴀᴛᴇ ᴡɪᴛʜ ᴀ sᴛʀɪᴋɪɴɢ ᴍᴏᴅᴇʀɴ ᴅᴇsɪɢɴ. Tʜᴇ ɢʟᴏssʏ ʙᴇᴀᴅᴡᴏʀᴋ ᴄᴏɴᴛʀᴀsᴛs ʙᴇᴀᴜᴛɪꜰᴜʟʟʏ ᴡɪᴛʜ ᴛʜᴇ ᴍᴀᴛᴛ ᴡᴏᴏʟ ʏᴀʀɴs ᴜsᴇᴅ ᴛᴏ ᴄᴏᴠᴇʀ ᴛʜᴇ ʙᴀᴄᴋɢʀᴏᴜɴᴅ. Tʜɪs ᴛᴇᴄʜɴɪQᴜᴇ ᴡᴀs ᴠᴇʀʏ ᴘᴏᴘᴜʟᴀʀ ɪɴ ᴛʜᴇ ɴɪɴᴇᴛᴇᴇɴᴛʜ ᴄᴇɴᴛᴜʀʏ ꜰᴏʀ ᴛᴇᴀ ᴄᴏsɪᴇs, ᴄᴜsʜɪᴏɴs ᴀɴᴅ ᴄʜᴀɪʀ ᴄᴏᴠᴇʀs. Usᴇ ᴛʜɪᴄᴋ ʙʟᴀᴄᴋ ᴘᴀᴘᴇʀ ꜰᴏʀ ᴀ ᴘʜᴏᴛᴏɢʀᴀᴘʜ ᴀʟʙᴜᴍ, ᴏʀ ʟɪɢʜᴛᴇʀ-ᴡᴇɪɢʜᴛ ᴄʀᴇᴀᴍ ᴏʀ ᴡʜɪᴛᴇ ᴘᴀᴘᴇʀ ꜰᴏʀ ᴀ sᴘᴇᴄɪᴀʟ ᴅɪᴀʀʏ.

1 The background is worked in tent stitch. Double a length of tapestry wool through the needle and knot the ends together. Insert the needle from the right side into the canvas and bring it out 2 cm (¾ in) to the left. To make a stitch, insert the needle into the hole diagonally below and to the right, then bring it out of the hole immediately above.

2 Work a few stitches until the end of the wool is covered, then snip off the knot.

3 Continue stitching in rows, following the chart at the back of the book. Leave a wide border all around and gaps for the beadwork motifs. Merge the shades of green as shown.

◄

## MATERIALS AND EQUIPMENT YOU WILL NEED
Tᴀᴘᴇsᴛʀʏ ᴡᴏᴏʟ, ɪɴ sʜᴀᴅᴇs ᴏꜰ ɢʀᴇᴇɴ • Tᴀᴘᴇsᴛʀʏ ɴᴇᴇᴅʟᴇ • 48 x 34 ᴄᴍ (19 x 13½ ɪɴ) ᴛᴀᴘᴇsᴛʀʏ ᴄᴀɴᴠᴀs, 10 ʜᴏʟᴇs ᴛᴏ 2.5 ᴄᴍ (1 ɪɴ) •
Eᴍʙʀᴏɪᴅᴇʀʏ sᴄɪssᴏʀs • Bᴇᴀᴅɪɴɢ ɴᴇᴇᴅʟᴇ • Mᴀᴛᴄʜɪɴɢ ʙᴇᴀᴅɪɴɢ ᴛʜʀᴇᴀᴅ • 2ᴍᴍ ɢʟᴀss ʙᴇᴀᴅs: ᴄᴏᴘᴘᴇʀ, ʟɪɢʜᴛ ʙʟᴜᴇ, ɢᴏʟᴅ, sɪʟᴠᴇʀ ᴀɴᴅ ʙʟᴀᴄᴋ •
Cʀᴀꜰᴛ ᴋɴɪꜰᴇ ᴀɴᴅ ʀᴜʟᴇʀ • Cᴀʀᴅ • Bᴏᴏᴋʙɪɴᴅɪɴɢ ꜰᴀʙʀɪᴄ • Pᴀᴘᴇʀ ɢʟᴜᴇ • Aᴅʜᴇsɪᴠᴇ ᴛᴀᴘᴇ • Bʟᴀᴄᴋ ᴏʀ ᴡʜɪᴛᴇ ᴘᴀᴘᴇʀ •
Hᴏʟᴇ ᴘᴜɴᴄʜ • Pᴀɪʀ ᴏꜰ ʙʀᴀss sᴄʀᴇᴡ ʙɪɴᴅᴇʀs

4 Thread the beading needle with beading thread. Stitch on the beads one by one, making a tent stitch in the opposite direction to the wool stitches – the beads will then lie in the same direction as the wool stitches.

5 Every four or five stitches, make two securing stitches to prevent the beads from unravelling.

6 Complete the beadwork, following the chart at the back of the book and using different colours of beads.

7 Cut two pieces of card the same size as the finished embroidery plus 10 cm (4 in) on the length. Score a line 10 cm (4 in) from the left-hand short edge on both pieces. To make the back cover, cut a piece of bookbinding fabric the same size as the card plus 2 cm (¾ in) all around and clip the corners. Glue the paper backing and press on to the card. Fold over the edges and glue down. To make a lining, cut a second piece of book-binding fabric the size of the card and glue inside the back cover.

8 For the front cover, lay the embroi-dery on the second card, lining up the right-hand sides plus seam allowance. Stretch canvas over card and tape edges to wrong side. Tape left-hand side of the embroidery to front of card. Cut a piece of fabric 12 cm (4¾ in) x the width of the card plus 4 cm (1½ in). Match to the edge of the embroidery and glue in place. Fold the fabric edges over the card and glue down. Line the front cover as the back.

9 Cut 40 pieces of paper 1 cm (½ in) less all around than the card. Mark position of the holes on the back and front covers and the paper, then punch holes. Place paper between the two covers, thread screws through layers and secure.

# SPIRALLED "CHANDELIER"

IN THIS DELICATE MODERN VERSION OF A TRADITIONAL GLASS CHANDELIER, DROPLETS OF COLOURED GLASS HANG AND QUIVER FROM A SIMPLE STRUCTURE OF SPIRALLED WIRE. SUSPEND THE CHANDELIER FROM THE CEILING WITH A LENGTH OF STRONG FISHING TWINE. TO SHOW IT TO BEST ADVANTAGE, PLACE IT IN FRONT OF A WINDOW OR CAREFULLY OVER A HANGING LIGHT SO THAT THE LIGHT SHINES THROUGH THE BEADS.

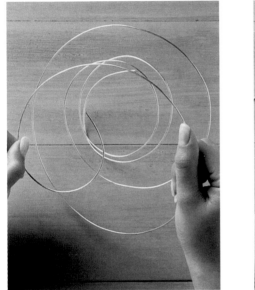

1 Using wire cutters, cut two lengths of the thick wire 120 cm (47 in) long. Bend each piece into a spiral.

2 Using the pliers, bend a small loop at each end of both pieces of wire.

3 Assemble the two spirals of wire together, as shown. ▶

MATERIALS AND EQUIPMENT YOU WILL NEED
WIRE CUTTERS • 250 CM (100 IN) OF 2 MM WIRE • ROUND-NOSED JEWELLERY PLIERS • 0.2 MM WIRE •
SELECTION OF SPHERICAL AND FACETED GLASS AND PLASTIC BEADS • SMALL GLASS BEADS • 4 MM (1/16 IN) BUGLE BEADS

4 To make the droplets, thread a piece of thin wire through a large glass spherical bead and a small bead – the small bead will act as an anchor. Pass the wire back through the beads and twist the ends together.

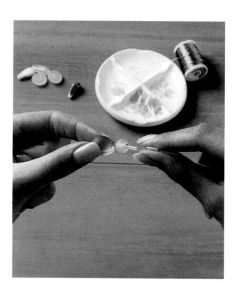

5 Thread on some bugle beads, then twist the wires to make a stem. Make about 30 droplets, using different beads in different arrangements.

6 Wind a short piece of wire on to each stem. Bend the ends into hooks, using the pliers.

7 Suspend the droplets at intervals on the spiral frame.

8 To hold the sprial shape, some of the droplets should be twisted over two rounds of the spiral.

9 Finish by adding glass beads on to the ends of the spiral frame.

# FLOWERED FRAME

DECEPTIVELY FRAGILE THREE-DIMENSIONAL STRUCTURES CAN BE MADE BY SIMPLY THREADING BEADS ON TO WIRE THAT IS TWISTED TO HOLD THE BEADS IN PLACE. MAKING BEADED FLOWER-AND-FOLIAGE CORSAGES, TIARAS AND BROOCHES WAS A POPULAR VICTORIAN PASTIME. MIX UP A FEW SMALL COLOURED BEADS AND USE TRANSLUCENT ONES INSTEAD OF OPAQUE TO MIMIC THE DELICATE HUES FOUND IN NATURAL PETALS AND LEAVES.

1 To make the leaves, cut 22 cm (8¾ in) of 0.4 mm wire. Twist a small knot in one end to stop the beads falling off. Mix up a few pink beads with the yellow. Bend the wire in half, thread on 18 beads, push up to the bend, then twist the wire together to form a beaded loop.

2 Wind the working wire around and down the stem 5 mm (¼ in), make another loop and thread on 18 more beads. Wrap the working wire around the stem another time and make another loop at the same level. Make 2 more pairs of loops along the length of the stem. Twist the wire around the stem.

3 Cover the twisted stem by wrapping it with floss thread.

## MATERIALS AND EQUIPMENT YOU WILL NEED
WIRE CUTTERS • 0.4 MM BEADING WIRE • ROUND-NOSED JEWELLERY PLIERS • SMALL WHITE, PINK, YELLOW GLASS BEADS • FLOSS THREAD • DRILL AND SMALL DRILL BIT • WOODEN FRAME • PROTECTIVE GOGGLES • 0.2 MM BEADING WIRE

4 Cut 40 cm (16 in) wire to make small flower, 50 cm (20 in) for large. Bend wire 10 cm (4 in) from one end, make a small circle. Twist to form frame. Pick up a few pink beads with the white, thread 24 for small flower, 30 for a large.

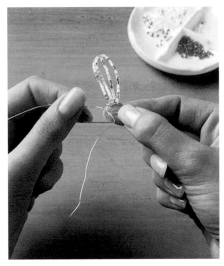

6 Thread on beads, then twist the wire around the top of the loop. Thread on 16 beads to make a small flower and 24 for a large flower.

8 To make the centre, thread on 12 yellow beads and twist a half spiral. Push the working wire through the centre and twist it around the stem.

5 Make a loop by twisting the working wire around the circle.

7 Add more beads and twist the wire around the spiral frame. To make more petals, make four more loops positioned around the spiral frame.

9 Position bead flowers and leaves, mark these points and drill holes.

▶

**10** Push the wire stems of the beaded flowers and leaves through the holes and twist them into a knot on the wrong side of the frame.

**11** Trim the wire. Using the thinner wire, secure the knots on the wrong side of the frame.

# BEAD CURTAIN

THIS EXOTIC WINDOW DECORATION IS DESIGNED TO MAKE THE MOST OF THE BEAUTIFUL INDIAN LAMPWORK BEADS USED. THE LIGHT FILTERING THROUGH THE CURTAIN INTENSIFIES THEIR COLOUR AND INTRICATE FILIGREE WORK. ALL THE BEADS ARE GLASS WHICH MAKES THE CURTAIN VERY HEAVY, SO IT IS IMPORTANT TO MAKE EXTRA FASTENING-OFF STITCHES. THE CURTAIN DOES NOT HAVE TO COVER THE WHOLE WINDOW; THREE-QUARTER LENGTH WOULD LOOK VERY EFFECTIVE. YOU CAN ALSO MAKE A CURTAIN FOR A DOORWAY, USING PLASTIC BEADS INSTEAD OF GLASS FOR SAFETY.

1 Measure the desired width of the curtain and cut the wood to fit. Mark points 2.5 cm (1 in) apart and 2.5 cm (1 in) from the edge, as shown. Drill holes at these points.

2 For every hole, cut a length of fishing twine to double the desired length of the curtain plus 60 cm (24 in). Thread both ends through the hole then through the loop and pull taut. Try to keep the loops untangled.

3 Working from left to right, thread on the following beads: (length 1) eight blue and one lampwork, (length 2) 12 blue and one lampwork, (length 3) 16 blue and one lampwork, (length 4) 12 blue and one lampwork. Repeat sequence to complete the width of the curtain.

4 For row 2, again working from left to right, add 16 blue beads and one lampwork bead. For row 3 add 12 blue and one lampwork. For row 4, add eight blue beads and one lampwork bead.

5 For row 5, add four blue, one green, two blue, one green, one blue, one green, one blue, 12 green, a lampwork.

6 For row 6, add 20 green and a lampwork. On alternate strands, add three green and a pendant. Pass all strands back through last beads. Finish with a knot below last lampwork. Knot each strand up through itself, make seven more knots. On alternate strands, add a green bead. Pass strand back up through penultimate bead. Make several finishing knots.

MATERIALS AND EQUIPMENT YOU WILL NEED

TAPE MEASURE • SAW • WOODEN PICTURE RAIL, AT LEAST 5 CM (2 IN) WIDE • PENCIL • DRILL AND FINE DRILL BIT • FISHING TWINE • SCISSORS • 5 MM (³⁄₁₆ IN) BLUE OVAL GLASS BEADS • LAMPWORK BEADS • 5 MM (³⁄₁₆ IN) GREEN OVAL GLASS BEADS • LARGE GLASS PENDANTS

# WATERFALL SCREEN

SHIMMERING DROPLETS OF WATER APPEAR TO CASCADE DOWN THIS STUNNING MODERN SCREEN. THE EFFECT IS CREATED BY TRANSPARENT PLASTIC CRYSTALS, SUSPENDED ON FINE SILVER EMBROIDERY THREAD. USE BEADS OF DIFFERENT SIZES TO GIVE INTEREST TO THE DESIGN. THE MACHINE EMBROIDERY THREAD CAN BE USED DIRECT FROM THE REEL WITHOUT THE NEED FOR A BEADING NEEDLE OF ANY KIND. MAKE THREE MATCHING PANELS, FOR A FREE-STANDING SCREEN.

1 For each panel, cut two pieces of wood 140 cm (55 in) long and two pieces 40 cm (16 in) long. Sand thoroughly.

2 Place the two short pieces across either end of the long pieces. Position the brackets on the inside of each corner and mark the position of the screws. Using a drill bit to match, make holes at these points. Screw the brackets in place.

3 Paint the panel with two coats of white emulsion and leave to dry. Paint the spheres with two coats of silver paint and leave to dry.

## MATERIALS AND EQUIPMENT YOU WILL NEED

SAW • 11 M (12 YD) OF 5 X 5 CM (2 X 2 IN) WOOD • SANDPAPER AND SANDING BLOCK • 12 RIGHT-ANGLED BRACKETS AND SCREWS •
DRILL AND DRILL BITS • SCREWDRIVER • PAINTBRUSH • WHITE EMULSION PAINT • 12 WOOD SPHERES, 7 CM (2¼ IN) DIAMETER •
SILVER PAINT • HAMMER • LONG NAILS • 1 CM (½ IN) DIAMETER PLASTIC TUBING • 6 HINGES • 12 SCREWS • DOWELLING
TRANSPARENT PLASTIC CRYSTAL BEADS, IN VARIOUS SIZES • 2 REELS SILVER MACHINE EMBROIDERY THREAD • SMALL SILVER GLASS BEADS • SCISSORS

4 Hammer in a nail 3 cm (1¼ in) from the top and bottom on the inside edge of each side strut.

5 For each panel, cut two pieces of plastic tubing 45 cm (18 in) long and push over the protruding nails.

6 Mark the position of the hinges on the side edges of the panels, 30 cm (12 in) from top and bottom. Check that the screen will fold, then screw in place.

7 Mark the position of the spheres at the four corners. Cut four pieces of dowelling 5 cm (2 in) long. Drill holes in the frame and the spheres with a drill bit the size of the dowelling. Push dowelling into the spheres, then into the frame.

8 Thread the transparent beads in random sequence directly on to one of the reels of silver thread. Leave 10–30 cm (4–12 in) gaps between groups of beads, knotting thread after each group.

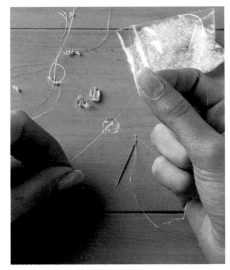

9 Thread on a plastic bead then pass the thread through the bead again. Thread on small silver glass beads in groups of three or more. Fasten off the end of the thread and cut.  ▶

**10** Unravel a little thread from the other silver reel. Tie one end to the lower piece of tubing on the first panel. Pass the reel over the tubing at the top, then under the lower tubing. Continue back and forth across the width of the panel.

**11** Wrap the beaded thread around the tubing in the same way. Repeat with the other panels.

# FRINGED LAMPSHADE

GLASS BEADS ARE AT THEIR MOST BEAUTIFUL AND MAGICAL WHEN LIT FROM BEHIND. EVEN A PLAIN PAPER SHADE CAN BE TRANSFORMED WITH A LONG BEAD FRINGE. THE SEQUENCE OF BEAD COLOURS VARIES SLIGHTLY, TO TIE IN WITH THE HAND-PAINTED STRIPES AND ADD EXTRA INTEREST. IT IS IMPORTANT TO USE A GRAPH PAPER GUIDE SO THAT YOU CAN CHECK THAT EACH STRAND OF BEADS IS THE SAME LENGTH.

1 Draw freehand stripes of varying widths down the length of the lampshade. Leave to dry.

2 Using a sharp needle, pierce a row of holes 5 mm (³⁄₁₆ in) apart just above the bottom rim.

3 Cut yellow thread twice the desired length of the fringe plus 25 cm (10 in) and double through the beading needle. Pass the needle through a hole on a yellow stripe, then loop through and pull taut.

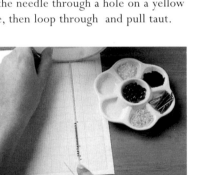

4 Mark bead sequence on graph paper. Thread on small beads: 11 cm (4½ in) of yellow, one purple, one yellow, one purple and one yellow. Add a bugle, then alternate five small yellow and four purple. (On alternate strands, add an extra two of each colour.) Add three yellow.

5 Add one purple teardrop and three yellow beads. Insert the needle just below the purple teardrop and make a fastening-off stitch, checking that no thread is showing. Pass the needle up the strand.

6 Make a fastening-off stitch below the bugle then pass it up through the bugle and make another fastening-off stitch. Pull gently on the strand to remove kinks. Continue around the shade. For the white stripes, use white thread and substitute transparent beads for yellow ones.

MATERIALS AND EQUIPMENT YOU WILL NEED

YELLOW OIL-BASED MARKER PEN • TUBULAR WHITE PAPER LAMPSHADE • TAPE MEASURE • SHARP SEWING NEEDLE • SCISSORS •
YELLOW AND WHITE BEADING THREAD • BEADING NEEDLE • PENCIL • GRAPH PAPER • SMALL YELLOW GLASS BEADS • SMALL PURPLE GLASS BEADS •
4 CM (1¾ IN) PURPLE BUGLE BEADS • PURPLE TEARDROP BEADS • SMALL TRANSPARENT GLASS BEADS

# BEADED TASSELS

Tʜᴇsᴇ ʙʀɪɢʜᴛ-ᴄᴏʟᴏᴜʀᴇᴅ ᴛᴀssᴇʟs ᴀʀᴇ ɪɴsᴘɪʀᴇᴅ ʙʏ ᴇᴛʜɴɪᴄ ʙᴇᴀᴅᴡᴏʀᴋ. Sᴛɪᴛᴄʜᴇᴅ ᴛᴏ ᴇɪᴛʜᴇʀ ᴇɴᴅ ᴏғ ᴀ ʙᴏʟsᴛᴇʀ ᴏʀ ᴛᴏ ᴀ ᴄᴜsʜɪᴏɴ, ᴛʜᴇʏ ᴡᴏᴜʟᴅ ᴄᴇʀᴛᴀɪɴʟʏ ᴀᴅᴅ ᴀ ɴᴏᴛᴇ ᴏғ ᴅʀᴀᴍᴀ ᴛᴏ ᴀɴ ɪɴᴛᴇʀɪᴏʀ ᴅᴇsɪɢɴ sᴄʜᴇᴍᴇ. Fᴏʀ ᴀ ᴍᴏʀᴇ ᴇʟᴇɢᴀɴᴛ ʟᴏᴏᴋ, ᴜsᴇ ᴛʀᴀɴsʟᴜᴄᴇɴᴛ ᴏʀ ᴍᴇᴛᴀʟʟɪᴄ ʙᴇᴀᴅs. Tʜᴇ ғɪʀsᴛ ᴛᴡᴏ ᴛᴀssᴇʟs ʜᴀᴠᴇ ᴛʀᴀᴅɪᴛɪᴏɴᴀʟ ᴡʀᴀᴘᴘᴇᴅ "ʜᴇᴀᴅs", ᴛʜᴇ ᴛʜɪʀᴅ ᴜsᴇs ᴀ ʟᴀʀɢᴇ ʙᴇᴀᴅ ᴀs ᴛʜᴇ "ʜᴇᴀᴅ". Cʜᴇᴄᴋ ᴇᴀᴄʜ sᴛʀᴀɴᴅ ᴀɢᴀɪɴsᴛ ᴀ ɢʀᴀᴘʜ ᴘᴀᴘᴇʀ ɢᴜɪᴅᴇ ᴀs ʏᴏᴜ ᴡᴏʀᴋ.

**1** For the turquoise and red tassel: cut a piece of tape 25 cm (10 in) long. Mark the desired length of the tassel on graph paper and the colour sequence. Thread the beading needle and fasten on at one end of the tape. Repeat the following sequence all along the tassel: thread on 18 small turquoise beads, eight red beads, then one large and one small turquoise bead.

**2** Using the last bead as an anchor, pass the needle up through the second-to-last bead then all the way up the strand. Insert the needle into the tape and make a stitch to one side. Repeat along the length of the tape.

**3** Roll up the tape and secure the tassel with several stitches.

## MATERIALS AND EQUIPMENT YOU WILL NEED

Sᴄɪssᴏʀs • Fᴀʙʀɪᴄ ᴛᴀᴘᴇ • Pᴇɴᴄɪʟ • Gʀᴀᴘʜ ᴘᴀᴘᴇʀ • Bᴇᴀᴅɪɴɢ ɴᴇᴇᴅʟᴇ • Bᴇᴀᴅɪɴɢ ᴛʜʀᴇᴀᴅ • Sᴍᴀʟʟ ᴛᴜʀQᴜᴏɪsᴇ ᴀɴᴅ ʀᴇᴅ ɢʟᴀss ʙᴇᴀᴅs •
Lᴀʀɢᴇ ᴛᴜʀQᴜᴏɪsᴇ ɢʟᴀss ʙᴇᴀᴅs • Sᴇᴡɪɴɢ ɴᴇᴇᴅʟᴇ ᴀɴᴅ ᴛʜʀᴇᴀᴅ • TᴜʀQᴜᴏɪsᴇ ᴇᴍʙʀᴏɪᴅᴇʀʏ ᴛʜʀᴇᴀᴅ •
Mᴇᴅɪᴜᴍ ʀᴇᴅ ᴄʀʏsᴛᴀʟ ʙᴇᴀᴅ • Sᴍᴀʟʟ ᴡʜɪᴛᴇ ᴀɴᴅ ʟɪɢʜᴛ ɢʀᴇᴇɴ ɢʟᴀss ʙᴇᴀᴅs • 2 ʟᴀʀɢᴇ ᴏʀᴀɴɢᴇ ɢʟᴀss ʙᴇᴀᴅs • Sᴍᴀʟʟ ᴅᴀʀᴋ ɢʀᴇᴇɴ ɢʟᴀss ʙᴇᴀᴅs •
Tᴡᴏ ᴍᴇᴅɪᴜᴍ-sɪᴢᴇ ʟɪɢʜᴛ ɢʀᴇᴇɴ ɢʟᴀss ʙᴇᴀᴅs

4 Fasten on with embroidery thread and wrap tightly around the "head" of the tassel. Fasten off securely.

6 For the looped green and white tassel: plan an even sequence of colours on graph paper. Cut a 25 cm (10 in) piece of tape and fasten on with beading thread, as in step 1. Thread on the following beads: 13 white, seven green, 24 white, seven green, 13 white.

7 Insert the needle back into the tape at the same point to make a loop. Make a stitch to secure, then make a stitch to one side. Repeat along the length of the tape. ▶

5 Fasten on with a beading needle and thread, at the top of the bead "skirt". Thread 15 small turquoise beads to cover curve of the "head". Insert needle into the top and bring it out at the bottom. Pass needle through last bead threaded, thread on two fewer, take over curve and through last bead at top. Insert needle from top to bottom, repeat sequence to cover "head". At the top, pass needle through the "head" and another 20 small beads, then back through "head" to make a loop. Fasten off.

*Below: Beaded tassels can be used in jewellery or interior design for instant added detail.*

**8** Complete the "head" of the tassel as in steps 3–5, adding a large red bead at the base of the loop.

**9** For the green and orange tassel: mark the desired length of the tassel strands on graph paper. Cut thread double this length and thread on four small light green beads. Using the last bead as an anchor, pass the needle through the first three beads to fasten off. Thread on small beads: 20 light green, 40 dark green and 24 light green, adjusting the numbers to fill the strand. Using the last bead as an anchor, pass the needle through the second to last bead, then through the entire strand, making finishing-off stitches all the way along. Make eight more strands in the same way.

**10** Cut a length of thread, double it and thread the ends on to the needle. Fold the beaded strands in half and tie the thread loop around all the strands at this point. Pass the thread ends through the large orange bead. Thread on one medium light green crystal, 17 small light green beads, one medium light green bead and 17 small light green, then pass the needle back through the orange bead to make a loop. Fasten off.

# TEMPLATES

NEEDLEPOINT PHOTOGRAPH ALBUM

CHILD'S SLIPPERS

WOVEN BRACELET

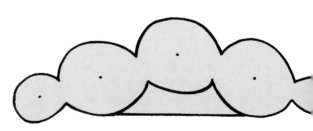

PEARL TIARA

# SUPPLIERS

**United Kingdom**
The Bead Shop
43 Neal Street
London WC2H
Tel: (0171) 240 0931

Ellis and Farrier
20 Beak Street
London W1R
Tel: (0171) 629 9964
*Beads and trimmings*

Beads
259 Portobello Road
London W11
Tel: (0171) 792 3436

Hobby Horse
15–17 Langton Street
London SW10
Tel: (0171) 351 6951
*Beads and trimmings*

John Lewis
(consult your telephone
directory for nearest branch)
*Wide range of sewing
equipment and materials, fabrics and sewing
machnes*

**Canada**
Dressew
337 W Hastings Street
Vancouver, BC
682 6196
*Sewing and craft materials*

**Australia**
Lincraft
(stores in every capital city except
Darwin). For store addresses telephone
(03) 9875 7575

Spotlight
(60 stores) Telephone freecall
1800 500 021

# ACKNOWLEDGEMENTS

**AUTHOR'S ACKNOWLEDGEMENTS**
I would like to thank the following contributors for their beautiful projects: Victoria Brown, Pearl Tiara; Judy
Clayton, Wrapped Earrings and Wallet; .Lucinda Ganderton, Venetian Necklace, Drawstring Bag and Milk Jug
Cover; .Daniella Zimmerman, Dramatic Painted Gloves, Velvet Bolster Cushion, Spiralled "Chandelier" and
Waterfall Screen.

Thanks are also due to Peter Williams for his patience and excellence.

**PICTURE CREDITS**
The publishers would like to thank the following for permission to reproduce pictures in this book: Christies' Images: p 8
Native American beaded cloth sash, p 9 gloves of white kid embroidered in silver thread and sequins; The Embroiderers' Guild: p 10
Victorian Berlinwork waistcoats, photographer Julia Hedgecoe, p 11 charts, samplers and slippertops in Berlinwork, photographer
J. Hedgecoe; the printed silk voile dress on p 11 is reproduced courtesy of the Trustees of the Victoria and Albert Museum.

# INDEX

album, needlepoint, 72–4
amber beads, Chinese
 necklace, 26–7

bag, drawstring, 59–61
bead looms, 20, 25
beading needles, 20
beading thread, 18
beading wire, 18
beads, trading with, 8
beeswax, 20
Berlinwork, 11

blackberry button, 32–3
bolster cushion, velvet, 56–8
bone beads, Chinese necklace,
 26–7
bookbinding fabric, 18
bottle collar, 65–7
bracelets:
 cord-beaded bracelet, 36–7
 woven bracelet, 43–5
brushes, 20
bugle beads, 16
 child's slippers, 63–4
 fringed lampshade, 88–9
 spiralled chandelier, 75–7
buttons, 18
 blackberry button, 32–3
 encrusted jewels button, 34
 flower button, 33–4
 tassel button, 34

candle-holder, bead, 68–9
canvas, tapestry, 18
chandelier, spiralled, 75–7
child's slippers, 63–4
Chinese necklace, 26–7
Christmas decorations,
 38–9
collar, bottle, 65–7
cord, 18
cord-beaded bracelet, 36–7

cotton balls, 18
 Christmas decorations, 38-9
couching, 24

cover buttons, 18
craft knives, 20
crimping beads, Venetian
 necklace, 28–9
crystals, 16
 waterfall screen, 84–7
curtain, bead, 82–3
cushions:
 bead-trimmed cushions, 52–5
 velvet bolster cushion, 56–8

devoré scarf, 40–2
dramatic painted gloves, 48–9
drawing pins, 20
drawstring bag, 59–61
drop beads, 16

earrings, wrapped, 30–1
embroidery hoops, 20
embroidery scissors, 20
embroidery threads, 18
encrusted jewels button, 34
equipment, 20–1

fabric markers, 20
fabric paints, 18
fishing twine, 18
floss thread, 18
flower button, 33–4
flowered frame, 78–81
found objects, 16
frame, flowered, 78–81
fringes, 22–3
 drawstring bag, 59–61
 fringed lampshade, 88–9
fusible bonding web, 18

glass beads, 16
gloves, dramatic painted, 48–9

graph paper, 20
"grisaille work", 11

history, 8–11
hoops, embroidery, 20

interfacing, 18

jewellery findings, 18
jewellery pliers, 20
jug cover, 70–1

knives, craft, 20

lampshade, fringed, 88–9
lampwork beads, 16
 bead curtain, 82–3
 Chinese necklace, 26–7
leather, dramatic painted
 gloves, 48–9
lill pins, 18
looms, bead, 20, 25

loops, 24
loops with stems, 24

marker pens, 18
materials, 18–19
metal beads, 16
milk jug cover, 70–1
millefiori, 16
muslin, milk jug
 cover, 70–1

natural materials, 16
Ndbele-speaking
 people, 8
necklaces:
 Chinese necklace, 26–7
 Venetian necklace, 28–9
needle-woven beading, 24

bottle collar, 65–7
needlepoint photograph album,
 72–4
needles, 20

"Opus Anglicum", 9

paintbrushes, 20
painted gloves, 48–9
paints, fabric, 18
palettes, 20
patchwork, 11
pearl beads, 16
 pearl tiara, 50–1

pearlized sequins, 13
photograph album, needle-
 point, 72–4
picot, bead, 22
pin boards, 20
pins, lill, 18
pliers, 20
pottery beads, 16
pre-strung beads, 16

ribbons, 18
 wrapped earrings, 30–1
rocailles, 16
rulers, 20

scallops, 24
scarf, devoré, 40–2
scissors, 20
screen, waterfall, 84-7
semi-precious stones, 16
sequins, 16
 Christmas decorations, 38–9
 devoré scarf, 40–2
sewing machines, 20
slippers, child's, 63–4
spiralled chandelier, 75–7
stems, loops with, 24
stone beads, Chinese

necklace, 26–7
stringing pre-strung beads, 22

tape, 18
tape measures, 20
tapestry canvas, 18
tapestry wool, 18
tassel button, 34
tassels, beaded, 90–3
techniques, 22–5
threading a bead loom, 25
threads, 18
tiara, pearl, 50–1
trading, with beads, 8
tweezers, 20

velvet:
 devoré scarf, 40–2
 velvet bolster cushion, 56–8
Venetian glass beads, 16
Venetian necklace, 28–9

wallet, 46–7
waterfall screen, 84–7
wax, 20
wire, beading, 18
 bead candle-holder, 68  9

flowered frame, 78–81
velvet bolster cushion, 56–8
wire cutters, 20
wool, tapestry, 18
wound beads, 16
woven bracelet, 43-5
wrapped earrings, 30-1

Zulus, 8, 36